Coins
on the
Track

(Newly Revised Edition – March 2019)

A Young Boy's Story of the 1950's and 60's South

by
David Allen Brooks

Edited by: Donna Fisher
Cover Design: Mark Brooks

---

*"I have never enjoyed reading a book
any more than I did this one."*
- Don Vaquero -

*"David Brooks captures the essence of growing up in
small town Georgia in the 1950's and 60's."*
- Linda Hutchins Pendergrass -

*"A unique talent in descriptive surroundings make for putting the reader
right at the location they're reading about."*
- Susan Sharpe Dickens -

Dedicated
to my beloved
Mother,
Nina Mary Burton Brooks

and to
the love of my life,
Jane Newman Brooks

Preface and Acknowledgements

This little book has been years in the making, believe it or not. Mostly, in my head. Often, I would sit for hours and even days, trying to come up with the right words. Then again, several months would pass when I would give it no attention at all. Ultimately, I've tried to tell it as I've lived it, some of the events from about 1955 to 1967.

For privacy sake, most non-family names have been changed. However, every event in the book actually took place, at least to the best of my recollection. Meaning that a few occurrences might certainly contain a small amount of "poetic license."

Thankfully, I've been the recipient of much encouragement. Many thanks go out to my family and friends who have read these pages and provided a push here and there.

To my wife, Jane Newman Brooks: Thank you for the patience and love you continue to provide me, and your great ability to "tell it like it is," as I wrote. Your knowledge as a wordsmith has been invaluable. My partner. My heart.

To my sisters Sandra Brooks Brady, Marilyn Brooks Willis, Dorian Brooks Dillard and Karen Brooks Henderson: Thank you for being in my life, and for providing so much of the content of this book, together with your kind words of love and support. You will always be in my heart.

To my brother, Jack Burton Brooks: Thank you for providing so much of the content as well. It is our many brotherly adventures and misadventures together that make up a great deal of this book. You honor me by reading this manuscript and with your continued love and support. You too, will always be in my heart.

Much appreciation and sincere gratitude go to the many friends who provided editorial and moral support, especially dear friends Donna Fisher, Mary Alice Sanders and Chris Barbieri. Donna Fisher especially gave much of her time and knowledge, providing the majority of editorial expertise.

Most of all, thank *you* for your interest in this book. You too, honor me by allowing me to share a little of my life and the adventures of a young boy growing up in a small Georgia town.

If I can bring you one smile, or perhaps just one small tear, then I have succeeded.

And finally, this: It is impossible to tell a story involving the prejudice and racism that was part of the 1950's and 60's South, without using the awful word "nigger." Rest assured, I find this word offensive to the extreme, but necessary to accurately tell certain parts of the stories herein. When possible, the phrase "n-word" (or n----) has been substituted. But, to properly communicate the profound ignorance that sometimes pervaded my little community, I have, at times, spelled it out. Today, I cringe when I hear the word, and even when I write or read it, no matter its context. I trust and hope that you can understand.

And, if not, forgive.

Home in Carl

He rarely looked up. With each stride, it seemed that time stood still. No worries. No ills. Nothing over which to fret. The grainy, gray-sectioned sidewalk was slowly being gobbled up with each of his tiny steps. He knew every section of it. Every crack. Every rise and fall and pitch and wail of it. He had walked it hundreds of times before. This sidewalk, this town, and in fact this very state were in his blood. He had been raised to be proud of who he was. What he stood for. He was home. And *at* home in Carl, Georgia.

Whistling, sometimes singing, he felt the weight of three large textbooks and his "Nifty" notebook tugging downward, aching his right arm. Switching the books to the other arm, he slowed a bit to time his step and perfectly kick an eye-catching stone lying near the sidewalk's center. It glistened in the mid-afternoon sun, almost as if it was sweating as much as he. It called out to him. Now the game was on. How far could he kick his newfound friend and keep the little rock within the confines of the walkway? One, two, seven, twenty? His personal record was thirty-three. Or was it?

Oh, the simplicity and innocence of kicking a rock. Of blue jeans and US Keds. Flat-topped hair with just enough butch-wax to make the front stand up as straight as grass blades. And wearing his favorite soft, t-shirt, the only hole-less one from the three-drawer dresser he shared with his brother, Jack.

The sidewalk ran alongside Highway 29, on the south side of the road, from west Auburn to the Superette in Carl, Georgia.

In 1906, Carl had been named for a baby boy born to a prominent couple, the Pates, who owned a general store and barbershop in the area. Prior to that time, it was named Dillard's Cross Roads and then Lawson before finally becoming Carl. Auburn was its larger, neighboring community, doubling in size to Carl, named for the rich, red soil of the area. Not that there was any less of the red clay in Carl. Auburn's size was nothing to brag about either. All through the 1950s, Carl's city limits sign read, "Welcome to Carl pop. 301." Auburn's residents numbered something over 500.

The boy was proud to say he was from Carl. He relished its smallness. Its homey, quirky residents, and the days spent roaming up and down the friendly confines of its sidewalk, its fields, and the railroad tracks that split the town and its county of Barrow perfectly in half. Whenever he played an imaginary basketball game on his dirt court in the back yard, it was Carl vs. Auburn, with him counting down the seconds before sinking the winning basket for underdog Carl. (And the crowd went wild!)

Sweat gleamed off his forehead as he neared home. He sensed the sticky moisture under his arms. He knew that it was sweat that made him who he was. The son of a carpenter. The son of a steadfast, loving mother. A Brooks boy.

It was hot. In fact, it seemed that growing up in the north Piedmont of Georgia, it was always hot. Very hot…or deep in winter, very cold. The boy's home was never air conditioned, and only centrally heated long after he would reach high school age. Home sat no more than twenty-five feet from the highway and proudly proclaimed itself as the first (or last) house in Carl. Directions were never a problem when sharing his locale with a friend or newcomer. "Just head east and we're the first house on the right after the city limits," he'd say proudly.

He walked past small homes owned by families such as the Smiths, Elliotts, Banks, Hunts, Simpsons, Clacks, Hawthornes, Haymons and Millers. He knew every resident. Who lived where, how many family members, and each one's particular personality and vocation.

Carl held very few secrets. Nor seemingly, did it want to. It was important to know *everyone*. To care about *everyone*.

The walk home from school this day was much like every other day. Yet the monotony of it all went unnoticed. It was the monotony after all that gave a certain sense of security and comfort. Care free and worry free. That was Carl in the 1950s.

Topping the last rise with home in sight, he hesitated by the wild plum tree at the corner of his side yard, beside the driveway. The plums were green still, as hard summer had not yet arrived. "Lord, could it get any hotter?" he thought to himself. He reached out and picked a plum or two and began to suck on its tart juiciness. The little treat exploded in his mouth. Frowning from its harsh taste, he spat out the seeds onto the highway watching it bounce off the steamy asphalt, and continued on.

A quick turn right, a few steps onto the concrete path formed by his Dad, through the aluminum screen door and front porch, and he was home. The smell of rutabaga filled his nostrils. And as hot as it was outside, it was hotter still, inside. He could hear the pressure-cooker filling the air with its mighty whistle. He hated rutabaga. Detested the smell of it simmering on the stove. And he knew he would have to force them down at supper that evening.

Passing the den, he tossed his books through the doorway leading to "the boys" bedroom. Jack's books were already there, crumpled against the headboard. One lay open on the floor nearby, having missed its mark. His worn and used texts landed perfectly against the two pillows wrapped neatly under the bedspread, where they would stay until after "playtime" and supper.

"David? Is that you?" His mother called out.

"Yes ma'am. What's for supper?" as if he didn't know.

"Rutabaga, your favorite," she said with a smile, her voice echoing off the kitchen's back wall, knowing all the while it most certainly was not. "But don't you worry, I'm warming up some Irish stew and cornbread from last night."

"Ah, sweet relief," he thought. His mother's stew was to die for. Irish potatoes, carrots, strings of beef with celery and onions, all smothered in a delicious sauce. And cornbread: bread of the gods. His mood shifted. Sweet goodness, his mother's Irish stew.

David was the youngest of six children in the Brooks household. There were four girls followed by two boys, Jack being his older brother by more than three years. Their shared bedroom just off the den, the boys slept in a bed that had once been occupied by older siblings Sandra and Marilyn, then Dorian and Karen, and now them. The old bed sagged in the middle, as there was no box spring for reinforcement. Neither he nor Jack really thought much of it. It was what it was.

Sandra being the oldest, almost sixteen years his senior, had long since moved out, married with children of her own. Marilyn, too, was married, and Dorian was in business school in Atlanta. Karen, the youngest of the four girls, was still at home, well into her high school years and occupied the back bedroom she and Dorian had previously shared.

There was also sweet Aunt Ruby, his Daddy's oldest sister, who lived next door and would join the family for dinner most every night. Years later, when space allowed, she would occupy the small back bedroom, where he and Jack had bunked.

Women surrounded Jack and David. It was from them that they would learn to love, respect and honor those of the opposite gender. Strong, Brooks women, each with their own special talent and personality, ran that household. Certainly, the boys' father may have *thought* he was the master, but it was his mother, aunt and those four girls who really ran things. Joe Brooks was the patriarch and enforcer, but the women were the managers.

This is the boy's story. But it's the family's story too. How a nucleus of nine -- six children and three adults -- could live and thrive during hard times. During sad times. And of course, during happy times. There's nothing spectacular about their stories. No one made history or broke any records. Just a north Georgia country family trying to make it, with many a friend and extended family member to help them along the way.

Thankfully, the happy times far outweighed the sad. That was Carl. That was the Brookses. And herein lies a small piece of their history. Together, with a small piece of *my* story, with them.

Warts and all.

~ 1 ~
Our Adventure Highway

We never gave it much thought, really. The old railroad tracks that played such a major role in our lives. At one time or another, all six of us, the Brooks siblings, sauntered along those tracks, usually in search of another adventure – in search of an unknown curiosity, only to be revealed during our walk.

Hardly an hour went by that those tracks didn't impact us in one way or another: we'd walk east or west along that shiny steel way, crossing them to visit a friend, balancing barefoot on the rails, chunking a bed rock at some innocent bird or squirrel, or have the train's deafening racket interrupt a front porch conversation. We'd curse its intrusion into our starry-eyed interest in a Yankees game on CBS or a favorite cartoon on Saturday morning. Adjusting the TV volume became routine. (I never remember ever having a television whose volume knob was intact through the life of the set.) The volume control occupied a special place on the bookshelves immediately behind the set. You knew exactly where to go to retrieve it, turn the volume up or down, and return it to its rightful home, bottom shelf, right by the yellow, bear-cubs flower vase.

What we would have given for a remote control, and the all-powerful pause button.

Counting train cars was an obsessive game with us, too. "I counted 112 cars the other day!"

"That's nothing. I counted 127. Top that!"

Never interrupt a young lad while he is intently marking each car in his mind, as the train passes from view. I'd wonder where these old steel cars had been. What mountains and rivers it must have crossed? What cities it had seen? Where it was headed?

There was one activity above all we enjoyed about the tracks: laying coins on the rails so as to be flattened and re-shaped from the weight of a 200-ton locomotive.

The trains careened down the tracks even on Sunday morning, that sacred time when all the Brooks children would rise, only to begin begging our parents to stay home from "church." We'd put on our best "Sunday clothes" to attend Sunday School and Worship. If the doors to Carl Baptist Church opened, you could count on Joe and Nina with their brood to be there.

Carl Baptist Church was a small, red brick, simple structure that sat on Carl/Cedar Hill Road near the main crossroads of the town. It had a tree-covered front, with very little grass, and a steeple that was as tall as the building was wide. The church sported a center aisle pulpit, with two sections of pine pews, nine pews to a side. It probably couldn't seat comfortably more than one hundred and fifty congregants. The choir loft stretched the full width of the sanctuary immediately behind the pulpit, with a curtained baptistery pool behind it.

That little church and its members provided me a social outlet, and was a witness as to how to behave, speak in public and act around same-age friends and adults.

No song or poem describes Carl Baptist any better than "Little Mountain Church House," by Carl E. Jackson and Jim Rushing:

> *There's a little mountain church*
> *In my thoughts of yesterday*
> *Where friends and family gathered*
> *For the Lord.*
> *Where an ol' fashioned preacher*
> *Taught the straight and narrow way*
> *For what few coins, the congregation*
> *Could afford.*

Dressed in all our Sunday best,
  We sat on pews of solid oak
And I remember how our voices
  Filled the air.
How mama sounded like an angel
  On those high soprano notes
When the roll is called up yonder
  I'll be there.

  Chorus....
Looking back now that little mountain church
  house
Has become my life's cornerstone.
It was there, in that little mountain church house
I first heard the words, I based my life upon.

At the all-day, Sunday singin',
  With dinner on the grounds
Many were the souls that were revived.
While the brothers and the sisters
  Who've gone on to Gloryland
Slept in peace in the maple grove nearby.

Written by: Carl E. Jackson & Jim Rushing
Lyrics copyrighted Universal Music Publishing Group
Lyrics licensed and provided by LyricFind

Carl Baptist sat a half-mile west of home, just as close to the town's railroad tracks as did our house. There was no escaping the noise of an approaching locomotive. Even on Sunday morning.

The train's clackety-clack-clack interrupted our preacher, Claude Healan. We always just called him "Preacher." He'd raise his voice in competition as the train approached; then as it clamored and coughed itself along side the church house, the walls and pews would shake, the lights would flicker, and we would sit motionless, observing Preacher pause, take a sip of water, and wipe his brow with an old, crumpled, overused handkerchief.

Then as the train would cease its thunderous roar, he'd continue like nothing had happened, never missing a beat. The train provided us children with a welcome break from his breathy phrases. A kind and generous man, he was one of my mentors during my early years, but I had a difficult time following the theme of his sermons. He used no notes, seemingly preaching what was on his heart each and every Sunday morning. Stopping on occasion to peer down on his pulpit Bible, he would read a few verses, take a deep breath for effect, then move on. His voice was deep and loud. I thought it must be how God sounded.

Preacher loved children, and he loved my parents. Daddy was always glad to see him pay a visit. Mother was a little less welcoming, as she was always overly concerned about the condition of her house, when unexpected guests arrived.

"Hide the playing cards! Dust off the coffee table! Pick up after yourself! Tuck the cigarettes in the sewing machine drawer!" You'd think Preacher had arrived wearing white gloves, for his regular household inspection.

Preacher and his wife, Miss Ann ~ *like true southerners, we called all adult ladies "Miss," whether they were married or not* ~ came over often for Sunday dinner. "Dinner" was what we now refer to as lunch. The evening meal was "supper." Our "fancy-eating" dinner table sat in the corner of the den, and was pulled out whenever dinner (or supper) was served. There were benches and chairs of every variety. I must have been 16 before I realized you could buy a "dining room set" with matching chairs.

This particular Sunday, there were eight or nine of us around that little table; Preacher was asked to say Grace, of course, and I thought he'd never finish that prayer. I was starving for some of that fried chicken and mashed potatoes. Okra, corn on the cob, black-eyed peas, lima beans, green beans. . . .You'd think the 7th Calvary had been invited. Actually, the 7th Calvary couldn't devour as much as we Brookses could put away.

During the prayer, my state of starvation became clear to everyone, as my stomach did triple half-gainer growls throughout. Jack elbowed me, as if I could do anything about it, and Mom peeked through her brow, giving me one of her patented, stern looks, followed by a faint smile. I thought to myself, "My gosh, will the man ever stop praying? Bless the stuff already! Pass the da'gone gravy! Let's chow down!

"Lord, we come to you today *(Lord, would you just look at that fried chicken)*, to ask you to be with us as we partake of this bounty *(man does that fried okra smell good)*. We beseech thee to bestow on us thy blessings *(we beseech thee to let this man stop praying)* this day and to watch over us. *(watch over us nothing, I'm watching the smoke rise from that perfectly formed cornbread)* And Lord thank you for all the other blessings *(would somebody get a hook?)* And on, and on.

By the time he'd finished, we'd prayed over brother Bartow's ulcer, Miss Angie's gout, Mom's wonderful ability to prepare a table, the weather, President Kennedy, the Cuban missile crisis, and the poor starving children in China. *(How about the poor starving children in Carl? And where's that blasted train when you need it!)*

When he finally pronounced "Amen." I sounded out right after him with a very loud and thankful "Aaa-MEN!" thankful, that is, that he had finally quit praying. Uh-oh, there came another one of those looks, except this time it was from Daddy – the MAN. Trouble would soon follow. How dare one of his angels embarrass him *IN FRONT OF THE PREACHER*, no less.

The railroad ran parallel with Highway 29, three or four good leaps from our house in Carl. With its aforementioned population of 301 in 1960, it meant our household made up 4% of the town's citizenry. We were so close to the highway, you could sit on the front porch and smell the diesel exhaust from a passing semi. Speeding transfer trucks caused the living room furniture to shake. The house would creak a little, and most of the paintings (purchased at Winder's Roses' 5-and-dime or Larry's EasyPay Tire Store) would require straightening.

While Carl was most certainly our home, I still today sometimes tell people I'm from Winder, simply because no one knows where Carl is. For that matter, most folks don't know where Winder is either. When I say I'm from Winder, my wife jokingly remarks, "Now you're just showin' off."

In winter, Daddy would cover the front screen porch with plastic in an effort to save Mom's precious houseplants. A passing car or truck made the plastic sheets balloon outward creating a noise akin to an opening parachute. If seeking out peace and quiet, the front porch was NOT the place to find it. Traffic and trains were as much a part of us as sweating in the summer and freezing in the winter. Most folks have seen ice on their windows, but have you ever seen ice on the INSIDE WALLS??!!??

It's a wonder that we were never struck by a passing vehicle. Mother would remark from time to time, "One of those big trucks is gonna come flying through our living room one of these days! And it'll probably be right in the middle of The Jackie Gleason Show!" *And awaaaay we go!*

Thankfully, she was wrong.

We called it "the train," "the track" or "the railroad." It was never known as the railway, locomotive or anything else to us. Officially, it was the CSX Railroad (Chessie Seaboard Expanded), but we just called it the railroad or the train. From our little farmhouse, after crossing the highway, then a shallow, weed-infested ditch, one found him/herself smack dab in the middle of those tracks. The tracks that coughed up a rumbling train three to five times daily, from Atlanta to Athens and back.

The "tracks" were our path. Our highway. Playing ball? Simply walk east, up the tracks, and there you were. Same thing for church, or visiting our play-cousins. We even built an extensive network of tunnels under the kudzu that grew wild along the sides of the tracks, providing us hours of entertainment, and plenty of ticks, chiggers and mosquito bites. There was never a shortage of this crazy plant along the side of the railroad, and beyond. It was everywhere. I always thought it should be our official "state plant."

Walking west could take us to school or to one of two stores in the neighboring village of Auburn, not to be confused with that "loveliest village on the plain" in Alabama. My best friend, David Smith, lived just across the tracks. I must have crossed them thousands of times to visit him.

Attempting to balance on the tracks was always a treat. Sometimes barefooted, we'd begin just across the road and start walking east toward Carl. If the rails were not too hot, balancing that half-mile stretch usually meant falling off once or twice.

"Don't fall off!" my older brother Jack would yell. "There's sharks all 'round. You'll be eaten alive, if you lose balance."

Memories are still fresh of the morning when the train derailed in front of our house, with one of the cars careening its way onto Highway 29. Fortunately, no one was hurt, but what a noise that morning.

I was sleeping soundly about 5:00 a.m. when this incredible noise shook my bed and the entire house. Much more than normal. Startled, I arose from bed, gathered my thoughts, and began to consider the possibilities: World War III, the Russians, Castro, a giant tornado? What on God's green earth could make that sort of commotion?

Still in my pajamas, I stepped out the front door onto the sidewalk. That old concrete pathway was always cold and grainy to my bare feet. But on this morning, its usual numbing effects on my toes were farthest from my mind. Eyes glazed over from sleep and with the morning fog and mist hanging above, I stared westward, detecting a huge billow of smoke wafting over the carnage. The train had obviously derailed with one car protruding skyward from the track bed. Other rail cars lay scattered along both shoulders. The odorous sensation of hot steel entered my head. I could smell what I thought to be brake fluid and motor oil. What little car traffic there was that morning began to stop alongside the road, partly from concern, but certainly out of curiosity as well. It was that time each morning for the slow and steady stream of commuters headed west toward Gwinnett County and Atlanta. I feared the worst, discovering only later that there were no injuries.

Returning to the house and preparing for the school day, I sat down to breakfast in the little kitchen just alongside the den and began to think about what had just happened. Slowly, yet like a bolt of lightning, it entered my head: Could I have been the cause of this?

As already stated, I, like my friends and siblings before me, loved to lay coins on the tracks. Mostly pennies, as a nickel was much too valuable. I could still buy a Coke for six cents in those days. In all my years of growing up in Carl, a dime was the largest denomination coin I ever saw squashed by a train. A quarter in your pocket practically made you the wealthiest kid in Carl. Twenty-five cents could buy a Coke, small bag of peanuts and a Zero candy bar, and you could still walk away with change. A Coke was six cents. Peanuts and a candy bar were a nickel each, and you had nine cents left over! How about another Coke and two Tootsie Pops? No problem.

Walking along the rails and hearing a train approach, we'd carefully place a shiny penny or two in the exact center of the hot steel rail. Standing to one side, we'd stare at the coin to try and detect where it bounced as the train's massive wheels made contact. Staring at the train's underbelly, it never ceased to amaze me how far the tracks would sink into the railroad bed as each pair of screeching wheels passed. Not once did I ever successfully see a coin smashed, or in what direction it flipped. The train would move away to destinations unknown, and we'd make our way up the gravel bed to begin our search. The staccato-clapping steel machine rolled out of sight as we wandered around the crossties and gravel, in search of our anticipated "prize." Never did I walk away from the tracks without finding my newly formed treasure. If it took hours, we'd press on in search of old flat Abe.

The prize meant an oddly shaped metallic piece with old Abe's or Tom Jefferson's head stretched beyond recognition. The coin was always a big hit at school. Showing it off to friends, we'd pass it around and stare at the funny indentions that had previously been on the coin's edge but now ran across one side. Abe Lincoln looked like "plastic-man" with his nose even longer than normal and his coif furled upward like some Mohawk do. After a few trips to school, and successfully hiding my prize from the pilfering fingers of my teacher, it would find its way into my underwear drawer, never to be seen again, or if found, tucked away again to join my other pocket occupants, like a marble, a buffalo nickel and plenty of pine straw and dirt. School friends who brought a flattened dime or nickel achieved instant fame. I immediately surmised that they were rich, having sacrificed such a coin. Not to mention that they were real risk-takers; it *was* against the law after all?

We Brookses were a little like those coins: sometimes shiny, other times dirty, changing, prized. Shaped and re-shaped. Seeking out some innocent but sometimes risky adventure, we were well behaved and for the most part well rounded in spite of our shortcomings. Mom and Dad made sure of it. We anticipated any opportunity to be something or someone we really weren't. "Let's play pretend" was suggested often. It was the simplest of times, growing up in the 50s and 60s. Yet, we yearned for something more. Surely, there was more to life than Carl, Georgia. Surely, life would hold more in store for us beyond this little hamlet.

One thing we were not, however. We were not children who intentionally caused harm to anyone else. For certainly without doubt, no jail, electric chair or hangman's noose could equal the punishment doled out by one Mr. Joe Jack Brooks. Daddy was our disciplinarian. Any false step was viewed as a personal affront to all he stood for. We were *not* to be an embarrassment to him or to his lovely wife, our mother.

A week after the big derailment, my cousin Mark Haymon and I were, what else, walking along the tracks in search of some harmless fun, when he mentioned he had heard the train derailment was caused by a coin on the tracks. The very thing that had entered my head that morning came hauntingly back to my mind. A little shaken and worried, I began to fret. Lord, could I fret, a wonderful characteristic implanted by my sweet Mother. If there had been a doctorate in worrying, she could have received it summa cum laude.

"No way." I remember saying. "There's no way a little coin weighing less than an ounce could cause a major accident involving a huge train. No way! Get real!"

"It's a federal offense, you know?" he replied. "The Feds are probably hangin' 'round Carl as we speak. What about that guy in the black suit we saw at O. E. Herndon's store yesterday? I bet he wuz a G-man! He looked just like Edward G. Robinson with that dark suit and tie! Plus he had that great hat on! He had to be one."

"You goofball! That was Randolph Lovin. He was on his way to his mother's funeral." I reminded him. (I would never confuse Mr. Randolph with Edward G.)

There never was an investigation. The Secret Service or FBI never arrived. I never saw anyone looking like a federal agent. Not even the Barrow County Sheriff made an appearance. I was off the hook. Yet another close call in the "story of the city." But I had learned my lesson. It was time for me to cease with coin smashing.

After all, if someone were ever killed or injured, I would have to face the ultimate penalty.

I'd have to face Daddy.

~ 2 ~
"Let Her Go, Willie!"

Day one of First Grade at tiny Auburn Elementary was uneventful for me. Well, sort of. Our live-in aunt, sweet Aunt Ruby, was Auburn's first grade teacher, and I had gone to school with her on several occasions before that year, visiting as a 4- and 5-year old. My Mother, sisters and Aunt Ruby had spent countless hours with me, reading aloud and teaching me to read. They helped make schoolwork easy and fun. It was a surprise for me to learn that not everyone in our First Grade class could read. I remember fondly how excited and eager I was to begin school, and to read. Still today, I have Mom, Aunt Ruby and four sisters to thank.

Nina Mary Burton was born on March 16, 1917 in Walton County, Georgia. She was the only child born to Eula Irene Miller and Charles Thomas Burton, also from Walton County, Georgia. Charles Thomas Burton was a son of Henry E. Burton (1860-1925) and Mamie A. Sheats (1866-1919) of Walton County. Charles Thomas Burton was born on January 3, 1892 in Walton County and he died there on December 18, 1917, not yet twenty-six years of age, leaving a young widow and his nine-month-old daughter, Nina. Eula Irene Miller was a daughter of

Mary Beatrice Hale (Hales in some public records, 1864-1935) and William Bertram Miller (1862-1925) of Walton County. Eula Irene Miller was born in Walton County on May 11, 1900, and died in San Lorenzo, California. She remarried William Burke after the death of Charles Thomas Burton, and on January 9, 1928, they had a daughter, Sarah Laverne (Polly) Burke. She later married for a third time, Gabriel Rosario. Nina Mary Burton died on December 10, 1988, and she and her husband Joe Brooks are buried in the Carl Baptist Church Cemetery in Carl, Barrow County, Georgia.

Nina was raised very differently from Joe, spending her childhood between Atlanta with her mother and sister, and Campton with her maternal grandparents. Her mother, widowed at an early age, was forced to work for their survival, and thus Nina matured quickly. At the tender age of eleven, Nina took care of a household and her baby sister Polly, while her mother worked, doing whatever she could. Her mother, at one time, was a nurse having come upon this occupation in much the same way Joe became a carpenter – self-proclaimed.

The Miller home in which Nina was raised still stands, across the road from the Campton United Methodist Church in Campton, Georgia. During her later years, Nina confessed that she was "spoiled by them" during those years, for they were very happy to have her as part of their family. Along with Eula Irene, the Millers had five girls, yet were still happy to have Nina "like one of their own."

Nina graduated from Monroe High School in 1935. She was in the school's Beta Club, French and Latin Clubs, and was a guard on the girls' basketball team, played in the days of three-on-three on each half-court. She was the salutatorian of her class at graduation, and just a few days after receiving her high school diploma, she was married.

During her early years of married life, Nina professed to know, in her own words, "nothing about housework, cooking or raising a family." But out of necessity and with a little help from friends and relatives, she learned quickly. She was a career homemaker, and put all her energy into raising children and creating a happy and healthy home atmosphere for her family. She was an excellent cook – especially home style vegetables, and she loved to sew, crochet and read. At one time, her personal library consisted of hundreds of books, many collected from her youth, all of which she had read. Also, she loved to write. Many of her thoughts and ideas became living words on "any old pad or notebook" which the kids happened to discard. One of her works entitled "For What It's Worth," chronicles her life from a very early age up until a few years before her death in 1988.

While at Carl Baptist Church, she taught Sunday School, directed the Vacation Bible School program and sang Alto in the Choir. She loved music of all types, and at any given time of the day (especially while house cleaning) she could be heard singing at the top of her lungs. She loved her life with Joe and her children, but probably yearned to travel more than she was ever able. Whenever an invitation was offered, she was ready to go, whether it was out to dinner with friends or out-of-state. She loved to trout-fish with Joe, and her patience far surpassed his. Many of her mid-life years were spent fishing and camping with Joe, especially countless trips with Otis and Margaret Haymon to Tallulah River and Rock Creek in the north Georgia mountains.

Her later years, after being stricken with kidney disease, caused her very little slow-down. She continued to travel as much as she could. She visited her children and grandchildren regularly and was active and independent up to her death. Nina Brooks was an amazing woman due to the fact that she unselfishly gave of herself in spite of her hard, harsh formative years. Her legacy is her simple *smile, her creativity, her special genius and her love of life, home and family. She was devoted at successfully raising a family, and in many ways personified the word "mother."*

For all those years prior to me attending school, my older siblings had gone off each day in the big yellow school bus, leaving me with mama, to be her "only child." It is strange to ever think of myself as an only child, when there were five other siblings in the family, but those days were often lonely and long. From a positive standpoint, I learned to play and entertain myself and to feed creative juices that would provide me a vocation much later in life.

I loved going to school. The prospect of making new friends made me very happy. The first day of school, I somehow was seated next to this skinny, freckle-faced, red headed kid who was very upset about being at school. I couldn't imagine why he was crying on his first day of school. His name was David Smith. David was at that time an only child, and someone who was probably even more tied to his mother's apron strings than was I, if you can imagine that. For I too was a pure mama's boy, but unlike him, I had my sweet Aunt Ruby right there to melt away any anxieties I might have had. David wanted to go home, and he wanted his mama…NOW!

I remember even as a 5-year-old that seeing people cry, adult or children, always bothered me, really impacted my psyche. It made me want to do something -- something to relieve his unhappiness. After all, shouldn't everyone be as happy as I? Besides, we shared the same first name. Maybe we should share other things too.

I reached in my new school satchel and pulled out a prized possession – my *Roy Rogers and Dale Evans Coloring Book* – what else, along with a fresh new box of 16 Crayola crayons. There was nothing like a new box of crayons to me, at that age. The way they smelled. Their perfectly carved points and unblemished wrappers. I would later be introduced to the "Giant 64-Crayon Box," which even had a crayon sharpener tucked away in the corner of the box. New colors, such as raw sienna, indigo, cerulean and turquoise. Crayons and coloring books were life's little elixir. Pushing the coloring book across his desk and holding up the crayons, I innocently asked, "You wanna color?"

His crying quickly subsided as he took the book and crayons, and began to thumb his way through the little box. Life's little elixir indeed. Thus began a friendship that would last through elementary school, high school and even college, as roommates at the University of Georgia.

We shared a love for the Atlanta Crackers, Live Atlanta Wrestling, comic books, baseball cards and reading. I still remember the first book that I ever read that didn't contain pictures or drawings: *"The Powerhouse Five," by William Heuman,* which he had read, and suggested to me.

I had never had a close friend my age. Until then, my only bud was my brother Jack, but he had gone off to school every day for the past three years. David filled that void to a tee. It quickly became evident that he was first of all, very smart. He didn't just keep up with me. He passed me. He was really good at reading, math and drawing. He seemed to do everything well. He became my gold standard.

My first overnight stay with a friend was with David. My first trip to the Dairy Queen in Winder, for a chocolate shake was with his parents. My first trip to a Crackers' game and later to a Braves' game was with David. He and I were inseparable. It's difficult to explain now what made us so close, besides our similar interests and shared name, but this friendship, though waned through the years, has always been there.

Something else we shared, though briefly, was a love for the same girl, Elaine Roarke. Elaine wore gorgeous clothes to school. Her hair was perfectly styled with beautifully formed ringlets hanging symmetrically around her rosy cheeks. She usually wore ribbons or cute berets in her hair. Her dresses were always folded just right and smartly clean. The crinoline petticoats under her lacey dresses rustled when she walked. Her ankle socks softly folded over embroidered edges were neatly tucked into her shiny patent-leather shoes. She had a turned-up nose and freckles, characteristics any fine, upstanding first-grader would fall for.

Not many weeks into the school year, I had even managed to sneak a kiss from her by telling her I had a secret, then instead of whispering it to her, I planted a good old smack right on one cheek, something that would probably get me thrown out of school today.

Our school's annual Halloween Carnival came around each autumn. Who can forget the Fish Pond, Cake Walk, the Spook-House and Bingo in the cafeteria? The Halloween Carnival was something really special. Like Christmas in October. We couldn't wait for it to arrive.

This particular year, Miss Hodgens, one of our teachers who farmed and raised horses, would volunteer to bring one of her smaller ponies for the children to ride. Her son Willie was given the job of holding the reins for each child and slowly ride around in a small roped off circle two or three times. A nickel got you "riding high."

I spied Elaine preparing to take a ride on Willie's pony, and slipped in line just behind her. Here was my chance to really impress her. After all, I had seen every episode of Roy Rogers' TV shows, along with Gene Autry, Hopalong Cassidy and the Cisco Kid. Riding a horse was going to come second nature to me!

I patiently watched as Elaine mounted the pony. Willie slowly led her around the designated circle several times, as she smiled cutely to her audience of waiting kids. She was a Princess on her steed. Eat your heart out Queen Victoria, Joan of Arc and yes, even Dale Evans.

Willie helped her off the little horse, directed her to the side exit area, and motioned me over for my turn on the pony.

I was ready. This was my time to shine. My chance to show Elaine what a professional horseman I was. She would be so impressed, that she would curtsy to my obvious horsemanship. My hour of power had come at last!

I placed one of my PF Flyers in the left stirrup and leapt onto the saddle, though not quite as smooth as Roy would have. Quickly finding the other stirrup and placing both hands on the saddle horn, I began to be led by Willie around the circle. A quick look to one side told me that she was watching. This was my chance. But how manly can a guy be when there's an older kid holding the reins? And me holding the saddle horn? Roy or Gene would never be caught dead in such a predicament.

Looking over the pony's ears, I remarked to Willie, "You can give me the reins, Willie. I know how to ride a horse. Just hand them over to me. I'll show you."

"I can't do that," Willie said, "My Mother would kill me. Besides, I've got strict instructions to lead the pony at all times."

"It's all right. I've been on a horse. I know what I'm doing. Just give me the reins." I lied.

Now the fact was, the only time in my life that I had ever actually ridden an animal was with my brother on the just-weaned calves we would bring home from our Uncle Emmitt's farm. They made great riding animals for a short while that is, until they became so big they could kick your brains in, or gore you to death. Rodeo rides on our bulls never lasted more than a few seconds, besides.

Willie gave in to my insistence and handed over the reins. Now I was a real cowboy! But something was still amiss. Looking down, I noticed he was holding onto the harness still. "You can let go, Willie. I know what I'm doing."

"I really shouldn't." he quickly came back. "I'd get in big trouble."

"No, really, you can let go. I'll be fine."

"No way, David. I can't get in trouble."

Now, I'm getting a little upset and very much embarrassed at being led around by this kid who is only a couple of years older than me. "Let her go, Willie! Let her go!!!" I exclaimed.

And so...he did.

My first wrong move was to drive my heels into the pony's sides. After all, I had seen Gene and Roy do that a million times. That's what cowboys do. The pony reared its head ever so slightly, as if getting ready to buck, and away we went. He soared through the ropes dragging a few orange cones with him, and took off for God knows where. I had never been on any carnival ride that was as fast, or as bumpy, or as unpredictable, as that little pony.

Like anyone who had never been on a horse, I held the reins about as high as my head with each rein in one hand about twelve inches apart. My first inclination was to grab the saddle horn and hold on for dear mercy, but what would Elaine think? Instead, I was rocking from one side to another, doing my best "drunk-rider" imitation. My backside was bouncing like mad, and both feet came out of the stirrups. Nonetheless, I held on, somehow staying on. As the pony picked up speed, I began to lose my balance backwards. My feet flew up higher than my head, and I felt my backside being swept by pieces of the pony's tail. I caught a glimpse of the crowd of kids, and especially Elaine, and gave my audience my best "I-meant-to-do-that" look.

I could hear the pony breathing now. My crossed-bats, "Little Leaguer" baseball hat flew off my head as both feet continued to rise up. I could see myself biting the dust any second, when much to my surprise, and relief, Willie caught up with us, grabbed the pony's halter and wheeled us around. I rose up quickly in the saddle, took hold of the horn, and did my best Gene Autry imitation by smartly crossing one leg over the pony's mane, sidesaddle. All I needed was Gene's guitar. My dignity, I thought, had been saved.

Looking down on Willie and maintaining my balance ever so smartly, I spied the crowd with Miss Hodgens standing among them. She was screaming bloody-murder at Willie for agreeing to let me ride on my own. I continued with my best Cisco Kid stance, one leg still bent across the top of the saddle and the other in its stirrup. If I had had "The Kid's" sombrero, I would have waved gloriously to the crowd. "Hey Pancho! You all right?" Part of me felt like I had just made the trick-ride of the century. The other part wanted to dig a hole and bury myself.

After jumping from my steed, I quickly retrieved my ball cap, running back to the line and crowd of kids watching and waiting patiently. As I passed Willie, I called out, "Hey Willie, can I come back and ride again?"

Willie didn't answer but gave me a look that would melt cold steel. I took that as a no.

Adding insult to injury, Elaine was nowhere to be seen. Guess she had witnessed authentic trick riding before and that my little excursion was no big deal. Looking around, I spied her, giggling with some other girls over by the library door.

"What could be so funny?"

To this day, I still can't explain why I had to ask myself that question.

What a numb-nuts.

"Numb-Nuts"
Third Grade - 1958

~ 3 ~
"You Gotta' Aim Lower Next Time!"

Ever since I can remember, I was afraid of Daddy. He was a muscular, yet lean man, about six feet in height, and probably weighed around one hundred and seventy pounds. To me, he might just as well have been six feet, ten and well over two-hundred. Most days found him in overalls, Union brand, complete with the hammer loop and multiple pockets. Arriving home from work, he would smell exactly like a mixture of manly body odor, sawdust and worn out Old Spice after-shave. He had powerful, sun-baked forearms and long, gnarly fingers covered with calluses.

Joe Brooks wasn't "one to speak much," but when he did, his children listened, mostly from fear, but also out of pure respect. In his older years, he walked with a stoop, coming about from years of lifting heavy wood doors and planks. He had a large nose, characteristic of the Brookses, and very little hair – mostly on the side of his head. He always gave me the impression of someone who was extremely strong-spirited, yet he would sit in his recliner each Sunday night, watch *Bonanza,* and cry. Mother would say, "Your Daddy would cry at grocery store openings." He was strong, tender hearted, soft-spoken, and the scariest man I ever knew. When he did speak, we knew to listen,…but good.

Joe Jack Brooks was the sixth child and third son of Anna Lee (Annie) Parker and William Allen Brooks of Walton County, Georgia. Total siblings numbered six boys and three girls. He was born in Walton County on August 5, 1912, and he died September 28, 1982. On June 1, 1935, also in Walton County, Georgia, he married Nina Mary Burton of Campton, Georgia.

Joe entered the U.S. Army as a Private (SN# 44129833) at Ft. McPherson in Atlanta, Georgia on April 28, 1945, drafted at age 32. He went through his World War II basic infantry training at Camp (later Fort) Rucker in Alabama. He was assigned to Company L, 414 Infantry Regiment at Ft. Ord, near Monterey, California. He received his Army honorable discharge on November 1, 1945 at San Luis Obispo, California at the close of World War II.

He was educated through the eighth grade at Monroe A&M school in Monroe, Georgia (near present-day Walker Park school). Though never one to excel in school, he was a hard-working and energetic young man. As a tall and lanky eighth grader, Joe was quite athletic. While participating in a Walton County "field day" event at Monroe A&M, he long-jumped over eighteen feet, – quite an accomplishment considering his age and the fact that he was bare footed. A coach from Monroe High School encouraged him to continue his studies and to participate in track and basketball, but his need to work at home in support of the family, and perhaps his lack of interest in studies, led him to quit school in 1926.

The greater part of his youth, Joe lived with his parents and siblings in a large white clapboard house which still stands today on the Nicklesville Road in Campton, Georgia. There, he assisted the family in a multitude of farm related chores including livestock and cotton growing.

As a young man, prior to his military experience. Joe became a carpenter. In the late 1930s, he applied for a job with a local construction crew in Atlanta, told them he was a carpenter, and went to work. In reality, he only had a few tools and a few books of instruction. The books that he used during those early years are titled "Audel's Carpenters and Builder's Guide" reprinted in 1943. With that he made a very long and successful career as a skilled finishing carpenter, working most of his life with The J. P. Womack Construction Company and Beers Construction, both based in Atlanta. During his 25+ years as a carpenter, Joe worked on hundreds of projects, which reflected the phenomenal growth of Atlanta. His experiences as a finishing carpenter included: The Piedmont Driving Club, C&S Bank on Monroe Drive, Atlanta-Fulton-County Stadium and Stadium Club, First National Bank office building (downtown), Wieuca Road Baptist Church, Hartsfield International Airport, the Georgia State Capitol building in Atlanta, Neiman-Marcus, the umbrella lounge at the Regency Hyatt Hotel, and Lenox Square Mall. One of his more famous accomplishments was the winding staircase at the Georgia Governor's Mansion on West Paces Ferry Road, Atlanta. He also spent part of his career working for the Tennessee Valley Authority and for the U.S. Government, at Wilmington Beach, North Carolina.

During his life, Joe Brooks was a giving person, working on countless projects for his family, friends and church. His work can be seen in the possession of all his children, as well as in the pulpit/choir area of the original Carl Baptist Church on Carl/Cedar Hill Road in Carl, Georgia. He also assisted with the construction and finishing work of the older Sunday School space located adjacent and to the rear of the old sanctuary. While living in Carl, Joe completely restored their home's exterior and interior, often utilizing the "scrap" wood discarded at many of his work sites. The den of his and Nina's home in

Carl reflected the style and design of the Piedmont Driving Club in Atlanta. The cabinetry work in the kitchen reminded one of Neiman-Marcus, and the bookshelves in the family room had an appearance similar to display shelves at Lenox Mall.

Joe and Nina were active members of Carl Baptist for more than twenty-five years. He held the position of Sunday School Superintendent for over eight years, was made a church deacon about 1953, assisting in the layout and upkeep of the church cemetery where he and Nina are both now buried.

Joe was an avid hunter and fisherman. While in good health, he would hunt quail, dove and rabbit. As a hunter, he was an excellent marksman and could "out-walk" both his sons. He raised a few cattle, chickens and pigs, and loved to garden. Later in life, when suffering from ill health, he hunted deer and spent a great deal of time trout fishing. He and Nina enjoyed their later years camping in the north Georgia Mountains. He loved to spend time with his grandchildren and to visit his children's families. Never one to travel too far from home for extended periods of time, however. Joe and Nina lived their early married years with the William A. Brooks family in Campton, where Nina was taught by her mother-in-law to cook and "keep house." They later moved to Winder and then Carl, Georgia.

Although a taskmaster (taking after his father), Joe also knew how to love. He was an affectionate man with his wife and children, often showing emotion through a tear or hug. Never fully educated himself, he recognized the importance of education for his children. Studying and excellence in school were very important to him. Though his wages were for the most part meager, he offered his children whatever they desired in continuing their education. All six children continued their education beyond high school.

Though he had very little formal education, Daddy always recognized the importance of education for his children. Good grades were an absolute. No excuses. B's and C's were met with stern words of consternation. D's and F's were totally unacceptable, and met with certain corporal punishment.

Growing up, I never saw him as a friend. It was years later, after I was married, that I began to have a real relationship with him. I could actually talk with him, being completely comfortable around him. I no longer viewed him as a threat. And I slowly came to realize how difficult it must have been to provide for such a large family, with little education and limited income. The pressures he must have felt.

Daddy loved to plant trees. It seemed that whenever he and Mama had a few extra dollars, which wasn't often, they would spend it on fruit trees, vegetable seeds and flower seeds. They would order seeds from a catalog, or simply visit the local "Seed-and-Feed" in Winder. He loved to plant and grow things he could eat. Mother loved to plant things she could simply see and enjoy. Working together, they made sure our yard held a plethora of fruit, vegetables and flowers.

Daddy especially planted pecan trees throughout our back and side yards. We had trees of apple, pears, peaches, and plums. We even had a small strawberry patch carefully planted in a sunny space between two pecan trees near the pasture fence. We also had two fig-bushes, one located above the septic tank, and another near the barn. Blackberries too were abundant on the edges of our yard.

I hated blackberries. Not the taste, mind you, but the times when Mama would give me a pail and tell me to fill it up. Blackberries meant chiggers, mosquitoes, gnats and briars, none of which God put on this earth for anything good. I would usually fill up my pail about halfway and then beg her to let me quit. Begging usually worked with me, because I could keep it up for hours, until Mama (or Aunt Ruby) would give in. I never once begged Daddy. I knew better.

"Mama, if you'll let me get out of picking these blasted blackberries, I'll be more than happy to buy you a jar or two of jam." That never went over too well with her.

Daddy hated blue jays. We had a huge pecan tree that stood about one hundred feet from our house. Its trunk was much bigger around than I could ever reach. Its lowest branches were bigger around than I was tall, it seemed, and the old tree reached far up into the sky. I was convinced it was the biggest tree in Barrow County. We swung from that tree, used its draping limbs as ladders to its upper reaches, and even tied a pulley system to hoist a newly harvested bull or pig. It was our cookout shade tree, slaughter tree, swing tree, and, more than anything else, our pecan tree, a tree ripe for the pickings by the local flock of blue jays.

It would put out thousands of small-shell pecans each October/November. Jack and I were given the task of picking up pecans – another chore that I detested. Picking up pecans, especially during a cold day, was thankless work, I thought to myself. And invariably as we picked them up, we could watch the blue jays fly in, grab a pecan and fly back out. To my way of thinking, they could have all they wanted.

But, not Daddy. He would shout at "those blasted jays" and immediately run and grab his 16-gauge pump shotgun. Standing on the back porch, he would spy one coming in for his next pecan, kick open the screen door, step out onto the top runner of the steps, aim and fire. He rarely missed. After an hour or two of this sport, there would be eight to ten blue jays lying dead under the old tree. I could only think about how many more pecans I would have to pick up due to their demise.

I had always heard how beautiful blue jays were. In fact, they were the state bird of some state, or somewhere, right? (Actually, they are not the state bird of any of our states.) So why in the world would Daddy kill such a beautiful bird?...Because they were terrorizing our pecan trees; that's why!

Always, before I turned five years old, we owned a milk cow – Bessie, being one. Bessie was a jersey cow with black tipped ears and tail. She was a lazy, old soul who was easy to pet; I would rub her soft hide, brushing away the flies and feel her cold, wet nose. Her ears were like velvet, and her eyes were hypnotizing. She was my pet, sometimes, when I had nothing else to do except stroll through the pasture and seek her out for some petting and "talking-to." Bessie gave us really good milk. Daddy would milk her each morning and evening and bring in a gallon or two for Mama to strain and immediately refrigerate. Some of it she would sell to neighbors for a quarter a gallon. But most of it became sweet goodness to the family and me.

I usually sat on the top rail of the wooden fence just outside the barn and watched, as Daddy would milk Bessie. She would be munching away from her feed trough, and Daddy would be bent over, sitting on his 3-legged stool squeezing away, as milk came squirting out each teat. It was something to see this as a four-year-old.

Occasionally, Bessie would "act up" and Daddy would stand up and slap her across the side. His voice was always deep, gruff and commanding. The cow knew, as did we, when he meant business. "Bessie! You bettah cut dat Out Now! Sit still and behave!" Bessie knew that if she didn't stop what she was doing, the next move was a swift kick in the side. Daddy didn't tolerate obstinacy from his children, but especially not from his animals.

On any given day, Bessie was really bad to reach her neck through the barbed-wire fence, trying to eat away at the grass in our backyard. You've heard of "The grass is always greener on the other side?" Well it couldn't be truer than with Bessie.

Our pasture was lined with old posts, many hand-cut years earlier. The barbwire was nailed to the wood, barbed across the top portion, and webbed below. Bessie didn't mind at all reaching through the wires to munch away at the beautiful clover on the other side. This usually meant the wire would be bent and the posts pushed aside, in time leading to cows getting out. What a nuisance, chasing cows in the dead of winter, or night, attempting to return them to their rightful place of grazing.

If Daddy happened to be outside and witness this, he'd usually pick up a rock and heave it at her, landing against her side with a "ker-thump!" She'd quickly pull her head back through, doing as much damage pulling back as working her way through. "Git-on Back, tha-ah, Bessie!" He'd yell. She'd take a quick glance at the "voice" and then just keep on eating. Then came the rock.

One breezy fall day, around 1955 or '56, the back door was propped open to capture as much breeze as possible, originating from the shady back yard. On days like this, every door and window in the house was open. Curtains flumed inward and flies would often make their way to the kitchen in search of a morsel. Mother hated flies with a passion. Sometimes, we would all be seated at the table eating lunch or supper, except for Mama, who would be waltzing around us, swatting flies, often with her dish rag.

This particular day though, Daddy was in his bedroom, just off the kitchen, when he spied Bessie again doing her thing. Two posts were leaning inward as she reached further and further, pushing the fence with her long neck and head.

I heard him explain, "That's it! I've had it with that dad-gum cow!" He immediately began to rummage through his closet. I knew he was looking for his gun. I remember getting really excited whenever Daddy got upset, that is unless I was his target. He brought out his 16-gauge and began loading as he scurried through the kitchen and out to the back porch. The familiar sound of the pump-action struck a nerve. I was extremely excited.

Bessie was our only milk cow. She was THE source for most everything good: sweet milk, biscuits, cornbread, rolls, cereal, cookies, cakes, milkshakes, butter and the like. Losing her would have been devastating to our little family's economy. Perhaps to our very existence, or at least I thought as much.

I could hear Daddy cursing and mumbling under his breath as he stepped very purposefully into the back porch. Our back porch was ten steps above ground and some fifty yards or so from the edge of the front pasture fence. It provided the perfect crow's nest for anyone who wished to pick off blue jays – or cows.

I followed Daddy step-for-step. As he propped the back screen door open and raised his gun, I held tightly to his tan work pants and braced for the jolt of the firearm. With arms wrapped completely around his leg, sitting firmly on one of his work boots, I closed my eyes, put both fingers in my ears and braced myself.

His eyes squinted. His arms and legs taut, steady and sure. I sensed him readying to pull the trigger.

Boom!

The shotgun fired into the afternoon air with a repeating echo across the pasture. Leaves from the big pecan tree shuttered as birds of all species took flight. The porch itself shook. My ears rang out with the sudden discharge of the shell. Daddy quickly pulled the gun lower and pumped the spent shell. It clanged onto the wooden porch floor, skipped a time or two and rolled down a crusty floor plank and out the door onto the yard below.

Bessie kept munching away on the tasty clover. Head down. Paying no attention whatsoever to Daddy, or to the noise.

"His aim is way too high." I thought to myself.

Setting up again, lunging his upper body into a shooting stance. Upright. Still. Steady.

"Boom!" went another shot. This time, Bessie pulled her head back through the wire fence, turned abruptly, and ran down the pasture valley and up the hill beyond. Lumbering, with her bouncing hipbones in perfect rhythm. Up, down. Up, down.

She was obviously spooked, but unhurt. Clear to me present day, his intentions were to scare Bessie enough to make her never want to stick her neck out again, no matter how green the grass.

I watched with heightened interest and excitement every little movement. Every gesture. Every huff and puff coming from the man. Then he looked down at me, and I at him. He let out a laugh of satisfaction; in his mind, he had succeeded this day. Laughter was part of our family's makeup, but rare in Daddy when it came to his children.

I didn't fully understand it all, but this I knew: the events I'd just witnessed were better than any episode of Roy Rogers or Gene Autry. My eyes were like saucers as I observed Bessie's tail flying in the wind as she scurried away. I thought how fortunate she must have felt to be saved by Daddy's awful aim.

I again looked up at him with great amazement. "You missed her, Daddy. You gotta' aim lower next time!"

~ 4 ~
Licking Away The Tears

As early as age three or four, I had a dog, or sometimes several dogs. Most dogs that I claimed were strays. Some scruffy, flea-bitten mutt would come strolling into our yard, and soon would be a "claimer."

The first dog was Cleo, or so I named her. Cleo was mostly a rabbit dog, that I later would learn was called a beagle. Cleo probably was owned by someone, but I quickly became her caretaker and provider. She was mine, because I fed her, petted her and scolded her when she needed it.

There were three lanes on our Highway 29, passing through Carl and Auburn. Two going east to Winder and one directed west toward Gwinnett County and Atlanta. As stated previously our home was only a few feet from the highway, as the living room and front porch would literally shake whenever a large truck would come by. And of course, just beyond the highway was the infamous railroad track. At night, a train would move the entire house. Over the years, however, the railroad became simply part of our living experience. If talking on the front porch and a train came by, we would just stop talking, wait patiently while the train passed, and then continue our chat, as it headed out of sight. Over lunch or dinner, the train's whistle and deafening rumble meant everyone was silent, with only the tinkle of silverware, tableware and drinking glasses. In a very strange way, our Carl home was a peaceful, yet often loud place in which to grow up.

I loved Cleo. She was a source of much fun and frolicking. She smelled to high heaven, had scabs all over her, was missing most of her teeth along with part of her left ear, but I loved her just the same. She may as well have been entered in the Westminster Dog Show in the Sporting Group. Cleo never complained. She loved to see me coming down the back steps. She would roll in the grass with me, lick me, and run with me across the pasture. We tumbled through the cool clover patches, played chase and fetch, and worked our way far through the back woods behind the pasture. She was mine. Her very existence depended on me, and me alone. I gave her dog food each day. Really nothing more than leftovers from dinner. That was her "dog food."

Cleo, and in fact all dogs, were never allowed in the house. We had no dog pen, and there was no way I could keep her tied up. What with the highway and the railroad, danger loomed over her wherever she went.

I had Cleo for no longer than a few weeks, when she turned up missing. I walked the back pasture calling for her, strolling up and down the sidewalks, hoping she would show. She was like most beagles in that she loved to roam. Constantly following her nose. Head and eyes down. Tail in constant motion. It was only after several days that I really began to worry about her. Where was she? Had she found a new home?

My usual walking territory, besides our property, included the aforementioned tracks. Balancing on the rail, my record was from the railroad crossing across the street from our house all the way to Carl Baptist Church. A good quarter-mile.

The railroad also meant encouraging the engineer to blow his whistle and counting the cars. Being able to report to a cousin or friend that you had counted a train with over one hundred cars was a major accomplishment. I became enamored with their clickety-clack, as it rolled along the tracks. There, just in front of our house was a changeover line, where one train could pull onto the sidetracks to allow another to pass, coming or going.

Trains would come in the night. I rarely realized they were there, after becoming so accustomed to their noise. I remember as a newlywed, when my wife and I spent the night with Mom and

Dad for the first time, a train came down the tracks, ninety-and-nothing. I was sleeping like a baby. Suddenly, my wife Jane sat up in bed as a train made its noisy trek alongside our house. "What the hell is that!!??" she exclaimed. "Go back to sleep, honey. It's just the train. I told you it would be coming along during the night." "Yeah," she said, "But you didn't tell me it was going to come through the living room!"

Trains were something we took for granted. They were part of our entertainment. Though none of us had ever worked for, or even been on a train, they were part of our soul.

I was a 3rd grader at Auburn Elementary when a student was sent to Miss House's classroom to fetch me. "The Principal would like to see David Brooks," said the 8th grader. My eyes quickly became saucers. My stomach was in my throat. A chill worked up my spine and I immediately broke out in a cold sweat. Being called to the Principal's office was the worst thing that could happen to me, in my brief existence. Not because of what the Principal might say or do, but what would surely happen once I got home. Facing Daddy.

I shakily removed myself from my little desk and walked to the door. I felt the eyes of all the students glued to the back of my head as if observing a prisoner on his way to the electric chair. I arrived at the classroom door and there in the hallway stood my brother Jack. He had this sheepish look, probably similar to mine. *We were both in trouble?* I couldn't believe it. Jack had the same fear of Daddy that I had. No trip to the Principal's office could ever be as bad as a trip to the clothesline, for a good whipping.

We walked down the hallway. It was all I could do to put one foot in front of the other. *Dead men walking.* Our heads hung low. I was absolutely scared to death. I had never been to the Principal's office for anything. Our escort had that look of "I'm out of class and I'm escorting the bad kids to their sentencing." Jack was almost in tears. So was I. "What did we do?" I asked him, as we trudged down the hall. "I have no idea!" Jack answered. Something told me that he really did know -- that *HE* had done something wrong, and I was called in as a witness for the prosecution. There was no way *I* could be in trouble. After all, I was the perfect child. Yeah, right.

We approached the door of Mr. Evanston, our old Principal. He probably was in his forties, though he may just as well been a hundred. "Come in, boys. Have a seat." It was like Dr. Frankenstein was about to perform lobotomies on two of his unwilling patients. We sat across the desk from the man. His white wisp of hair curved upward in front. His reading glasses rested low on his nose. He had that look I had seen many times before, whenever a "bad" kid was being corrected. His nose was red and rough from years of acne. Many of the kids called him "crater face." I just called him "Sir."

I melted into the seat, as did Jack, and we prepared ourselves for the verdict. I looked around the chair legs and arm rests for any tell-tell wires. Was this the "Auburn Elementary electric chair?"

"Ladies and gentlemen, have you reached a verdict?" "We have your honor. We find the defendants Jack and David Brooks guilty, and that they be sentenced to the fullest extent of the law." Like hanging from their necks until dead, for instance, or worse yet, meeting up with their Father.

Mr. Evanston looked us both over, cleared his voice and finally began to speak. The only thing I could figure was that Jack must have killed somebody, and the old man was calling me in as an accomplice.

"Gentlemen, we can't have students walking home from school on the railroad tracks," he said.

What!!! I thought to myself. We had been marched down the hall, humiliated in front of our classmates, and made to sit in the Principal's office to be told not to walk on the railroad tracks??? That was like not breathing. I was certain that never in the history of Auburn Elementary School had two boys been called into the Principal's office for such a silly charge. The fact was, most days, we would walk along the sidewalk from school. But, the railroad tracks always appealed to us. And on that one day we walked on the tracks, a teacher saw us, and decided to rat on us. Even Daddy was surprised that our little saunter had warranted such treatment.

I returned to class really puzzled. Even as a lowly third grader, I couldn't believe a principal actually wasted some of his time dealing with a "non-issue." Walking on the tracks!!!??? Good grief! "This is ridiculous!" I thought.

Who ratted on us? What teacher could possibly think that walking the railroad tracks posed any kind of danger? Could it be our sweet Aunt Ruby? Our sweet little old, first-grade teaching, hugging and kissing, sneaking us a quarter, talcum powder smelling, waddling down the path, sweet, sweet Aunt Ruby? How could she? Surely, it wasn't her.

Ruby Estelle Brooks *was born August 10, 1899, the oldest child of Anna Lee Parker and William Allen Brooks. She died December 3, 1989, at 90 years of age and was buried in the Carl Baptist Church Cemetery in Carl, Georgia. She was married briefly to Dewey Hogan on July 24, 1927, later divorced, but for most of her existence, she made a life as a single person.*

She was beloved as an educator in Gwinnett, Walton and Barrow counties. She began her career in a two-room rural school at Sorrells Springs in Walton County about 1918, there to remain until about 1923. There followed teaching assignments in Walton County at Campton and Double Springs, followed by a short stint in the Cobb County system, then on to teach in the Gwinnett County School System for ten years. She finished her career at Auburn Elementary School in Auburn, Georgia, retiring there in 1964 after a rewarding forty-five year career. She was afforded the opportunity to teach more than one thousand children, including three of her brothers, a sister-in-law, several nieces and nephews, and even great nieces and nephews.

"Miss Ruby" as she was known to her many pupils, also taught Sunday School to the five- and six-year olds at Carl Baptist Church for over twenty years. She loved to sew, was an accomplished cook, and was known to have read the Bible "cover-to-cover" at least three times. She was "famous" to her many nieces and nephews for having

countless books and magazines for children, and she afforded any child her time, in order to teach crafts, read or just tell a story. Her brothers and sisters called her "Boots." She also went by "Aunt Ruby," "Sweet Ruby," and "Ruby."

Although she never had children, she was considered a "mother" to hundreds of children in and outside the family, throughout the Auburn and Carl communities, for her entire life. Ruby Estelle Brooks carried with her an uplifting, happy disposition and was never known to speak an unkind word of anyone. She was a very special individual, and an inspiration to her family and to all who knew her.

One trait that was always held dear: "every niece and nephew in the Brooks family claimed that they were her favorites." What a legacy.

As it turned out, it wasn't Aunt Ruby who reported us to the Principal for walking on the tracks. Unfortunately, or fortunately for us, we never found out who the "stooge" was.

Jack and I loved those tracks. We each would pick a rail and away we'd go. Jumping from one rail to another was always a feat. Not just anyone could make such a leap and still maintain his balance.

Once, we were walking up the tracks headed toward Carl. Our baseball bat draped across one shoulder with the handle hooked through the glove's wristband. We would often whistle a tune. If a hot summer day, we dare not touch the blazing-hot tracks. Their heat would peel a layer or two right off the soles of our feet. We mostly whistled tunes from favorite TV shows or a hymn from "The Broadman Hymnal."

"Bringing in the (sheets) Sheaves" and the theme from Sugarfoot were favorites.

> *Sugarfoot. Sugarfoot. Easy Lopin',*
> *Cattle ropin' Sugarfoot,*

Carefree as the tumbleweeds, ajoggin'
Along with a heart full of song
And a rifle and a volume of the law....

We had not walked more than a half-mile when a distinct odor entered my senses. I had smelled that odor before when Dad had slaughtered a bull under the big backyard pecan tree. It was the smell of death.

Some twenty feet in front of us lay what was left of an animal. I could barely recognize it as being a dog. It seemed to have been torn apart from the inside out. That's what trains can do to a being when moving at full speed.

"It's Cleo!" Jack said. Bending down at the knees and staring at the bloody mess, I cried.

Having a dog or cat and keeping them for any amount of time were practically impossible. We were country kids. Walking a dog on a leash was not even something we considered. I dare say, we didn't know what a leash was.

And again, living next to a busy highway and railroad simply was not conducive to having pets. No dog pens. No security. Cleo most assuredly had experienced the dangers of living free…and dying.

What followed was and array of canine friends: June Bug, Moose, Shuffles, Humphrey and Bob, all suffering a similar fate. All bringing on the same tears.

Daddy had always been a hunter. He loved to hunt rabbits and squirrels. Later in life, he even enjoyed deer hunting with his sons-in law and occasionally with me. I was age twelve when Daddy brought home two of the cutest things I had ever seen. Daddy named them Sam and Sally, English pointer siblings and beautifully spotted with liver-colored markings perfectly placed about their heads and side. Their little tails wagged back and forth with blinding speed at the sight of Jack, Dad or me. They were to be the family pets, but as far as I was concerned, they were mine. Daddy put them in our barn, and soon spent several evenings and Saturdays building a dog pen around the barn. He even dug a trench for cement footings. The posts were treated with creosote, meaning these dogs were to be different. They were important.

Upon completion, Daddy cut an opening in the side of the barn, allowing them some inside covering for warmth, and relief from the rain or sun. I remember Jack and me taking a stick and writing all the names of my immediate family in the still-wet cement. Of course, I saved the cement in the doorway for mine.

I loved those dogs. Daddy saw them as a way to enjoy hunting. I saw them as my friends.

Sam grew to have a big blocked head. He was lean and muscular and always greeted me by jumping up on me whenever I entered the pen. Sitting on fence footings, he would nuzzle up against me, looking simply for one thing – to be loved. Sally was a little more aloof, only because Sam would nudge her aside. She was probably 15-20 pounds lighter than Sam, but just as loving. Her nose was a bit pointed. Both dogs' eyes glowed with unadulterated love and devotion. Most every day, it was a delight to see them, but I think more of a delight for them to see me.

It wasn't long before the dogs became a source of comfort.

I was a sensitive little guy. Being the youngest of six, it seemed that I was often the target of laughter. Most times, their aim was perfectly innocent in so many ways, but I felt it hurtful nonetheless.

One evening, I took it upon myself to announce to an after-dinner table full of folks, "Guess what, yawl. I can tell the difference between Sam and Sally!" The room erupted. I was simply and innocently referring to the shapes of their heads as the two grew and matured. What a stupid thing to say. I was mortified. Off to the dog pen I went, seeking consolation, and someone to lick away the tears.

I loved my brother Jack about as much as anything. Yet, we had some pretty horrendous fights. He always out-weighed me and was also quicker and smarter. Three and one-half years separated us; just enough for two boys not to see eye-to-eye. Our fights seemed numerous. Not really, looking back now. But one thing for sure resulted in each fight - back to the dog pen.

My dog pen ritual usually meant sitting on the footings of the fence, calling over Sam and Sally, and them licking the tears from my cheeks. They offered immediate solace for my miserable temporary melancholy. I would stroke their backs and heads, peer into those beautiful brown eyes and very soon feel better. Talking to them helped as well. "Hey, Sam. You love me, don't you? I want you to bite (fill in the blank) next time you see them. That'll show them not to pick on me. You too, Sally. Maybe if both of you could gang up on (whomever), that would finally teach them a lesson."

Both dogs would sit on either side of me, tilt their heads, and stare into my red eyes, as if to wonder, "Why are you so sad, old friend?"

Dogs are the most amazing of animals. I'm convinced they have souls. How could any living thing with such beautiful eyes not? I love what someone once asked me. "Do you know the difference between dogs and cats? Cats say, "You feed me, pet me, and take me to the Doctor. *I* must be God." Dogs say, "You feed me, pet me, and take me to the Doctor. *YOU* must be God." Although with only a few experiences I've had with cats, nothing could be closer to the truth.

I even loved their smell. Sam and Sally lived in a pen that was large by 1960s standards. It was probably thirty to forty feet square. The backside of the pen was reserved for them to do their business, so you can imagine the mess they made. I knew to stay clear of this area. But the front side was "our place."

One couldn't step into the pen without coming out smelling like wet dog, or at least as dirty. I'm thankful that God gave me multiple smells with which to deal. Therefore, "wet dog" wasn't so bad. To this day, giving my two yellow labs a loving hug, and inhaling, takes me immediately back to my days with Sam and Sally. Their love for me was relentless and selfless. They never demanded anything from me. Jack and I fed them once each day – a huge portion of *Jim Dandy* and table scraps. Not exactly the diet most veterinarians would recommend, but it's what we did.

Any time Sam and Sally were let out of their pen, they would run like mad around a large circle waiting for instructions. An old red ball or tennis ball were great toys for their retrieval-play. Sam would almost always outrun Sally, grab the ball and return it, eager to be petted and praised. Soon, their tongues would be practically dragging the ground, but they would always want more. They loved the water too. We would heave a ball far across

Wheeler's Pond, a small lake owned by a neighbor friend, the lake located some one-half mile behind our house. Sam and Sally would both leap in, pointing all four paws forward, belly flopping into the water. Both their little noses were aimed upward as they swam. One could see in their eyes that their little paws were paddling like crazy. They were great swimmers and adored the water. It was as much fun for us to watch as it was for them to experience. To Daddy, this was all part of the sporting life.

Sam and Sally were both great hunters too. Daddy and Jack were into hunting quail. Me, not so much. They would rise early on a cold morning, be fed a full breakfast by Mama, and off they would go. They'd return by early afternoon with ten or twelve birds, ready for dressing and for our eventual dining enjoyment. It's funny that as youngsters we would often eat wild game of assorted types like rabbit, squirrel, quail and dove. We even ate turtle soup on occasion. Delicacies all, now. Back then, just part of our usual diet.

Both dogs were great pointers. Though perhaps a little ill bred, they could point. God, how they could point. On the rare times that I went with Jack and Daddy, I was mesmerized by their pure athleticism. They could hold a point for as long as it took to approach and flush the covey. "Boom! Boom! Boom!" Shotguns would ring out and both dogs would then scurry to and fro, smelling for wounded game. They would scoop them up, bring them to Daddy and gently lay the bird in front of Daddy. Taking the bird and pushing it into his hunting vest's pocket, he would stroke the dogs' heads, pat them hard on the side and talk to them like they were his babies. They would look up admiringly as if he was God. They had achieved their rightful duty. Their job was done for now. Then away they'd go off on their next adventure seeking out another elusive covey of quail.

Sometimes in the middle of the night, Sam and Sally would start barking. If there was one thing Daddy treasured, it was his sleep. He could raise one heck of a holler when disturbed. Bouncing a rubber ball against the wall below his bedroom, playing under the pecan tree nearby, or barking dogs at night would really drive him crazy. He worked hard. Rest at night and a Sunday afternoon nap were precious commodities indeed.

"YOU BEDDAH' HUSH UP, NOW, SAM! HUSH UP AND GO TO SLEEP!" He'd yell from his bedroom window, which oh so inconveniently was on the same side of the house as was the dog pen. His opening and closing of his window and screaming out was generally what woke me up. Not the dogs. If they continued their incessant noise, the next move would be him slamming the screen door of the back porch, stomping down the ten steps to the back yard, and pummeling one of the dogs with a rock, or swinging away at the pen's fence with a bat-sized stick. If making contact with either, I would hear Sam or Sally yelp out, crying with pain and quickly retreating to the barn far away from their incensed owner. My little heart sank a little, knowing they might be in pain. We rarely heard from them any more on those nights when Daddy had to go out of the house to get them to quiet down.

It was Jack's and my job to feed Sam and Sally each evening. Sam was so dominating over Sally, we would feed Sally outside the fence and Sam in. They would devour the food with incredible speed. It was a case of feeding their stomachs, not their mouths. They couldn't have tasted a thing going down.

When Sally had reached about age two, Daddy decided to have her bred with another pointer in the Carl area. After agreeing to allow him to take the "pick of the litter," a Mr. Sneed drove his male pointer to our house and he and Sally did their thing in the barn. It excited me at the prospect of having an additional litter of pups in the pen. Dad's plans were to sell most of the litter and keep one or two.

I watched as Sally grew and grew, the puppies inside her doing the same. "She'll have a litter in about two months," Daddy had told me, not soon after her little encounter with the Sneed dog. I couldn't believe it. Two months? There's no way a dog can carry a full litter of pups, ten or twelve, in that short time. I thought this, but I knew not to question Daddy's wisdom on such matters. It was late summer when the pups were born. I happened to be in the barn, where Sally had been locked up and separated from Sam for the past week, when she began to give birth. I must have been about ten. It was an amazing thing to witness. She would get up from her "nest" that Daddy had prepared with hay and an old blanket, walk a few paces away, dip her butt low, and drop a pup or two. Then she'd carefully lick them clean of the afterbirth, pick them up with her mouth and place them back in the nest to begin nursing. After a few minutes, I suppose she felt the pain of birthing rise again and repeated the ritual. Each one looked more like rats than dogs. They were slimy, with eyes closed, whimpering ever so slightly. Incredible. The gift of life comes to dogs just like it does to humans.

In the days after her giving birth, Sally never once growled at me, while I sat and watched them nurse, squirming against her side. I would even walk over to the puppies and gently rub their noses or backs, even picking one up on occasions. Sally never protested. Today, I think that I had spent so much time with her that she truly felt like I was part of her pack, and that there was no way I was going to hurt her new babies. Picking up a puppy and staring at its drawn up shoulders and closed eyes, I soon would feel Sally's moist licks on my hand and her pup. It was like she was saying to me, "See what I did? Don't you love it as much as I do? Aren't you proud of me?"

There were eleven little puppies born that day. One would die soon after birth. I didn't know why, but it saddened me to see its tiny, lifeless body. I buried it far on the backside of the pasture in a small thicket of pines, carefully digging a hole, setting it in, and covering it with fresh topsoil, then pine straw. I couldn't help but think that day that I may have just buried the dog that would have been the best pet of all.

The noise they made was priceless. Almost like a purr or muffled cry. I thought they actually sounded more human than animal. There was a bond between Sally and her pups that was quickly formed that day. Very natural. Very planned. Something repeated throughout nature.

Sally would carefully "tip-toe" around her pups and slowly settle in around them. Her bloated teats would be jetting out, ripe for the pickings by these beautiful new creatures. I sat in amazement. My own little biology lesson right there in the hay of the old barn. Sally had done well.

After about six weeks, Daddy chose two of the puppies that were spotted in a butterscotch color and gave them to Gussie, our maid and her husband. As poor as we were, our church helped pay for a maid for us during Sandra's (my oldest sister) illness. Sandra suffered from a cancerous brain tumor, experiencing numerous surgeries and recoveries, each recovery less successful than the previous. Gussie would come to our house, and sometimes to Sandra's and iron, mop, and even at times clean windows. She was a sweet, soft-spoken spiritual soul who helped Jack and me in many ways,...but mainly helped Mama. It's a regrettable commentary on Black-White relations during the 60s that I never knew her last name. I think of her often still today.

All of Sally's other puppies were either sold or given away. Early on, I had chosen my "pick" of the two Daddy would keep. One of the males had perfect spots over his head and torso. He looked like a champion, and was one of the bigger pups as well. Whenever we would bring out a big platter of oatmeal and milk for the puppies, he was usually the one to dominate the others in getting his fair share. I even named him "Dollar" after the dollar-sized spots over each eye. He was a beauty.

When Mr. Sneed came over to take his pick, I prayed he would overlook Dollar, but it wasn't to be. I remember clearly the look on that puppy's face as old man Sneed cradled Dollar and claimed him as the "pick." Dollar didn't even look up at his new owner. His eyes stayed on me. They said, "Don't let him take me away. I wanna stay with you. I like it HERE!"

Mr. Sneed drove out the dirt drive and onto Highway 29, taking my Dollar with him. I dared not cry over a dog. At least not in front of Daddy. Later when I was alone with Sam and Sally, together with what was left of her brood, the tears flowed. I was confident Dollar was going to be a great hunter, and even better pet. I just hoped that old man Sneed would treat him well.

After a few more days, all the puppies were accounted for, each with new owners. We still had Sam and Sally, of course, but we had two of Sally's prettier puppies as well – one male and one female. I named them something, but to this day, I don't remember what. Daddy kept them for about six months and then discovered they were not making good hunters. They both were given to the man from whom Daddy had purchased Sam and Sally. I think he also had decided that we couldn't afford to feed four hungry dogs, especially two that were un-trainable. So again, we let dogs drift into and out of our lives. I don't remember the tears, but they probably came.

Sally was never the same after having that first litter. She became what Daddy called "gun-shy." Each time she would go out hunting, as soon as a gun would go off, she'd "turn tail" and run to Daddy's side, seeking comfort. Her hunting trips began to consist of staying right by mine or Daddy's side, seeking approval and love, while Sam sniffed back and forth up ahead of us, earning his keep as the family's hunting dog.

Eventually, after several trips like this, Daddy declared Sally useless and simply left her home, taking only Sam on hunting trips.

Most of my pre-adolescence and adolescence was spent with those two dogs. They saw me grow up and watched as I left for college. My interests in dogs waned as my interests in girls and having adult-like fun grew. Daddy grew older and sicker from a combination of influenza and heart disease, later with prostate cancer, which would take his life at age seventy in 1982.

A day in October of my second year at UGA, I came home to do some laundry. The weeds were noticeably higher in the dog pen, and its door was swung open.

By this time in his life, Daddy had become too old and too sickly to do much hunting anymore. His stoop had become much more noticeable. He coughed incessantly and easily tired. During overnight stays, I could hear him in the bathroom moaning and groaning to urinate, ravaged by prostate cancer. Hunting was no longer part of his life. He had grown old, weak, and more times than not, in major pain. It broke my heart to see this man whom I had once feared and later admired, wither away. His smile was gone. His gait was slow and measured. But he was hanging on.

"Where are Sam and Sally?" I asked Dad. "I returned them to their birthplace last week." He said. He had put them in his truck and driven them to Lawrenceville, where their original owner wished to continue hunting with old Sam, and breed sweet Sally, with perhaps another litter or two in her. They were gone as simply and as quickly as that. No fanfare. Not even a kiss of thanks goodbye.

I walked out to the empty dog pen, strolled among its tall weeds. There were small wads of dog hair drifting along the dirt pen floor. A dried-mud paw-print was evident here and there. I thought of all the times they had consoled me, licked away the tears, and pawed at me wishing to be petted and loved. I thanked them one more time. And, I cried one more time, this time, however, there were no lapping tongues to lick away the tears.

Thank you, Sam and Sally. You taught me the unconditional love dogs have for people.

People like me.

~ With Mama ~
Though grainy, it's my favorite photo.

~ 5 ~
Where Do Babies Come From?

I was a curious little cuss. From comments shared by my siblings and parents, I must have driven folks crazy with my non-stop questions. "What? Why? Who? And Where?" were the main portions of my vocabulary. I recall my older, married sisters and brothers-in-law growing very inpatient with me. Who can blame them?

The biggest curiosity: where the heck did we come from?

I was barely five years old, when my oldest sister Sandra was to give birth to her first child. Sandra was almost sixteen years my senior. Marilyn, sister number two, related to me that when Sandra found out that her mother was pregnant (again!), that she was mortified. After all, a sixteen-year-old in high school shouldn't have to explain to her cool friends that her parents were still "doing it." She even went several days not speaking to Mama. I'm confident I would have been of the same opinion.

I don't recall Sandra being pregnant, but I do recall being aware that a very special event was about to take place…and that I was to be an uncle.

Mom was in the kitchen. Big surprise. She was ALWAYS in the kitchen. My routine was usually to waltz in, grab hold of her apron strings and begin tugging until she would recognize my need for attention. Pulling on her apron, "Mama... Mama...... Mama, I need to ask you a question." Ignoring me, no response. After six children, I can only assume she was totally sick of questions from little ones. Later in life, she would recall praying to God, "God, why did you give me this one so late in life? He's about to run me ragged. Why didn't you give me this one first, when I was young and energetic?"

"Mama...Mama..." Still no response, I'd begin to poke her. "Mama!..."

"Davey, what on earth do you want?"

"Where do babies come from?"

Previous to my little kitchen visit and unbeknownst to her, I had already been to Daddy. Asking him this question only brought a very quick wave-off saying, "Boy, don't ask me questions like that." Or he might vaguely relate childbirth to the dogs or cows, which only added to my confusion.

Mama hesitated a little, rolling her eyes. "Where do babies come from?" I repeated.

Finally a response, "I don't know. Go ask your Daddy." How many times have parents used that come back, in the history of time?

Frustrated, I said, "Ah, Mama. It won't do no good. He don't know either."

My dear mother repeated that story at least a thousand times in her life. I've also heard it over and over from my sisters. I may have been the sixth and last child, but at least I was able to provide a little comic relief.

About the same time of year, I was out by the barn, "helping" Daddy replace a few clapboards that had rotted. The barn sat some 150 feet from the back of the house in the front corner of the pasture. A small feedlot was connected to its left, and a large Chinaberry tree flanked its right. Jack and I would often climb to the top of the barn and slide down the vertical tin roof sections only to grasp onto a large limb overhanging the barn. Our make shift swing set. What great fun, but what stupidity, especially on those days when the temperature approached 100-degrees and a slide down the tin roof meant one flaming toosh.

Daddy was always "fixing" something. I always thought it was because he was very hard working, and that he always wanted to be doing something to contribute to the family. Now, since having children and grandchildren of my own, I'm convinced he mostly wanted to escape the noise and madness that was children. Actually, it was probably a little of both.

Watching his muscles bulge as he swung a hammer or lifted a large board, I was impressed with his strength. He worked, walked, talked and smelled like a man. He was Superman in my little eyes. Never complaining about the job to be done, Joe Brooks certainly worked up a sweat, blowing a sigh when he was winded. This would become known as the "Brooks Huff" or the "Brooks Blow." Yes, I do it to this day, as does my brother Jack. I've even heard my two sons do it on occasion. Like father, like sons.

Daddy was hammering away at a new board, carefully placing it where the rotten one sat previous. I was mostly day dreaming, sitting on a low-hanging limb of the Chinaberry tree, watching him do his thing.

We had five or six bulls at that time. Daddy was a smalltime farmer, in that he had two gardens, each about 1 to 2 acres in size and several bulls that he would raise for slaughtering, and feeding the family. And there was Bessie as well, already mentioned as the family's milk source. Up to about age four or five, I also remember pigs and chickens as part of the "farm" animals.

On this particular day, the bulls seemed overly frisky. They were probably somewhere between six- and nine-months old. They were playing a bull's form of chase, and would sometimes go head-to-head in a game of "king-of-the-hill." Observing this activity, I noticed one of the bulls suddenly jump atop another bull from the rear and proceed to "ride him." I had never seen this kind of activity out of any of our livestock. It was a bull's way of attempting to dominate another.

"Daddy, what are they doing?" I quickly questioned. "Well son, don't you know? That's how babies are made." He answered, most assuredly.

Now, certainly never in the history of parenting and childhood has there been a more confused little boy.

I paused for the longest time, tipped my hat back on my head, scratched behind my ear and continued to watch. I was convinced more than ever that my Daddy knew nothing about where babies came from.

My conclusion was that my parents really WERE sick of having kids, because that's why we killed one or two bulls each fall. As long as we could keep the livestock population down, there would probably be no more new babies in the family. Simple logic. This would be my first understanding of birth control.

I said nothing. Just leapt off the tree limb and headed back to the kitchen.

Sibling number three was Dorian. Oh, how I loved that girl. My memories of Marilyn and Sandra are to this day out ranked by my memories of Dorian. She was beautiful. I recall her great smile and gorgeous hair. I even loved her name, a name that still today is very unusual. Dorian had several boyfriends, and lots of girl friends too. She was vivacious, energetic and talkative. Prior to attending school myself, I would sit in hers and Karen's room with my nose resting against the side window, peering eastward up Highway 29, anxiously awaiting the school bus that would bring my sisters home.

This ritual was repeated often, gazing westward, out the den window, in anticipation of Marilyn's visit with her husband Sid. It seemed like I was always pressing a window, breathing against the pane, drawing figures in the frosted glass. I knew very well what car to expect, what color it was, and that as soon as it was spotted, I'd be the first to run out the door to greet the new arrivals.

Like her mother before, Dorian married shortly after her high school graduation. And soon thereafter, she became pregnant with her first child, Hollie. She wasn't quite twenty years old and me barely nine when she was expecting. I watched in amazement as her belly grew and grew.

I must have been such a green, innocent nine-year-old by today's standards. In fact, innocent by any generation's standards. Such a goofball.

Back to the kitchen.

"Mama, tell Dorian to take that beach ball out from under her shirt." More ignoring. "I mean it, Mama, she needs to take that thing out! She looks silly."

Later during a visit to Dorian's apartment she rented with her husband, in northeast Atlanta, Dorian approached me for a hug. I was probably about as tall as her midsection. I reached out to touch her tummy. It was time for me to do something about this. Gently patting her swelling lower midsection, I demanded, "It's time for you to get that beach ball out from there. Give me that thing. I wanna play with it." Quickly lifting her maternity top and peering up under there only added to my confusion. "Where the heck is that thing?"

Everybody had a good laugh over that one. And they still do. My comedy material was really taking shape now.

Years earlier, when I fully realized the implications of Sandra having a baby, it dawned on me that *my* status may change as well. Back to the kitchen.

"Mama, when Sandra has her baby, what's my name gonna be?" My little mind wondered. More ignoring.
"Mama, what's my name gonna be?"

Finally a response, "Why David, of course. It'll still be David."

"No it won't!" I declared. "It won't be David!"

"Honey, yes it will. It'll still be David." "NO IT WON'T! IT WON'T BE DAVID!"

Slightly perturbed, "It WILL still be David."

"NO IT WON'T. IT'LL BE *UNCLE* DAVID! *UNCLE* David! That'll be my new name. Not just David."

What a knucklehead.

My family loved sweet, Georgia peaches, especially Georgia Belles, with their creamy white meat and scarlet centers. I loved eating them. But nothing made me break out in crazy hives like picking or peeling peaches. Mama and Daddy had a favorite spot in Cornelia, Georgia where they would take a summer day trip for peach picking. We would rise early on a Saturday, load up the Chevy and head north.

There was one particular farm in Habersham County where you could "pick your own," and save lots of bucks on the price of peaches. We'd return home, set up shop under the big pecan tree in the back yard and peel away. Bucket after bucket of peaches would be prepped for cutting into smaller pieces, or pickling whole. I could never understand the fascination of pickled peaches. Why in the world would you take a fruit as beautiful and tasty as a Georgia Belle peach and dip the thing in vinegar. Who was the first person to pickle a peach? They should be drawn and quartered.

Sitting on a variety of "outdoor furniture" pieces under the aforementioned pecan tree, we'd gather in a circle. Sweat beading and trickling down our faces, there'd be Mom and Dad together with Aunt Ruby, my youngest sister Karen (sibling #4), Jack and me. With each of us holding a small pail between our knees, and a "peeling knife," the cutting would begin. Flies were ever-present, especially with the sweet aroma of peaches. Wasps and yellow jackets were drawn to us too.

Gently making that first-cut near the tip of the peach, we'd run along the fruit's side, slowly spinning the peach in one hand and cutting with the other. Down and around the peach we'd go, leaving as much of the delicious meat as possible. If Mom or Dad saw that we were cutting too deeply and taking too much "meat" with the peel, they were quick to point it out.

Occasionally, I'd catch Mama pop a small piece in her mouth, so knowing it was okay, I'd do the same. It was sweet, sweet goodness. Georgia Belles: So much better than those "yellow-meat" Elbertas we would sometimes buy at Colonial Foods, the biggest grocer in Winder. Besides, "those old Elbertas probably came from South Carolina!" How dare another state try and steal our thunder. *We* were the Peach State, not *them*!

Years later, and much to my chagrin, I would discover that South Carolina produces more peaches yearly than does Georgia. "Has to be fake news," I thought, coining a phrase long before a certain President.

Somehow, with the great aroma and the treat of a peach wedge or two while peeling, I didn't seem to mind the itching quite as much.. Peeling peaches and preparing them as pieces for peach cobbler, with pound cake or cream, or as delicious homemade ice cream was great fun.

Often, we would float in and out of conversations, ranging from the weather, to what so-and-so said at church, to what a great crop of peaches it was that year. It was always a great crop of peaches, or so it seemed. Daddy would be wearing his customary cap with the giant swordfish on the front. I never understood why he wore that thing. He never went deep-sea fishing in his life. I think the man only saw the ocean once or twice – once on vacation in Savannah, and once in San Diego where he mustered out of the Army. But he loved that hat. As time progressed and he became older, the hats became more numerous. Soon the corner shelf of the kitchen above the drinking glasses was crammed with all shapes and colors of caps. You rarely saw him outside the house without a hat on his baldhead. Arriving home from work, Daddy would kiss Mama, remove his hat, placing it on the shelf just above the glassware, joining ten or twelve other hats, head to the bathroom to wash up and then sit at the kitchen table with his 64-ounce glass of tea. There followed three heaping teaspoons of sugar, the tinkling and stirring of his spoon, swirling and swirling the crushed ice and sugar just so, and supper could begin. I always thought, "Daddy likes a little tea with his sugar." All my life, every evening sharply at 5:00 PM, I witnessed this same routine, virtually unchanged.

Even something as simple as peeling peaches had its routine as well, including some great family "talks" or as my brother and I would call them, "talking-to's." Wishing to join in on the family-peeling conversation, I threw out a very thought-provoking question aimed at Daddy. "Daddy, are you and Mama kin?"

Now I had been pondering this for some time, and this seemed like the perfect time to ask. After all, they had the same last name. They must be kin. But someone once told me that you can't be kin and be married. This whole thing was a point of puzzlement to me, and I needed a clear answer.

Daddy stopped peeling. Looked across the circle at me and said rather briskly, "What kind of *FOOL* question is that? Good God Boy! Are you crazy?" (Today, the answer would be, "Why YES! Yes I was!")

Of course, none of that answered the question. It just made me feel embarrassed for asking. Mama rolled her eyes, and Aunt Ruby soon broke the silence, "Good gracious, David! Of course they're kin! A husband and wife are always kin!"

Daddy looked surprised at Aunt Ruby's answer. Mother just smiled, kept her head down and continued peeling. I wanted to dig a hole and climb in. Instead I just stuck out my lower lip, put my pail down and held off the tears until I could get to the dog pen for Sam and Sally to lick them away. Yet again.

So from that little conversation, I was certain that Mom and Dad must have been first cousins.

You know, growing up the "baby" can have its perks. But, by its very nature, you're babied right into being too sensitive. And, trust me, that I was. To my keen eyes and ears, everyone seemed to know more than me, do more than me, and be more than me. I was the stupid little kid, whose curiosity about life drove a hunger to know. This hunger would serve me well in many aspects of my later life, but mostly it would lead to trouble and embarrassment in my earlier years.

So, what was my final understanding of where babies came from?

Three choices: They either came from bulls riding one another, were disguised as a beach ball, or originated from two parents who were first cousins.

It's no wonder I was such a mixed-up, little kid.

~ 6 ~
Late for Supper

Barefooted was how one would find us in the summer. We walked "barefoot" through the pasture sometimes stepping in manure. We walked barefoot through the tiny springs that meandered through the back woods. We walked barefoot up and down the sidewalk, and even along those blessed train tracks.

Peering up or down the tracks one could see the waves of heat rising above the ground. Not only did the rails themselves sparkle and shine from the noonday heat, the surrounding gravel, cross ties and sand were equally hot. But, it didn't stop us.

The heat from the rails could literally scald the soles of your feet. We never stayed on them long. The cross ties, with their coating of creosote, were really hot too. A piece of wood from a roughly hewn crosstie could make a deadly, spear-like splinter. Enough to make you scream out, in pain. The gravel was completely off-limits even in mild temperatures due to its unevenness and jagged edges. The only place left was off to one side of the track bed where there was sand mixed with grass and weeds – passable to most.

Our house was constantly full of children and adults. With only one bathroom, we bathed every other day, but we would sit on the side of the tub and wash our feet daily. Even today, I can feel the coolness of the water rushing over my sun-scorched feet. Dirt was always worked in from the day's activities. Cleaning our feet made for some interesting odors along with incredibly dirty bath water. I was unaware of such hues of brown and green.

Going to bed with dirty feet was definitely something you just didn't do. I couldn't understand how the rest of our bodies could be soiled beyond recognition, but heaven forbid if you went to bed with dirty feet.

How many times did I stop whatever I was doing and ready myself for train car counting when its whistle approached. Trains would sometimes number well over one hundred cars. Any train that long usually meant at least three engines pulling them along, with perhaps one or two pushing from the rear, as well. At high speeds, counting could become a real challenge. Observing all the different logos on the train cars was both a fun and intriguing pastime, too. Later in life, as a student of graphic design, I would recall my first brush with art-as-design through the many images and designs on the sides of railroad cars. *Chessie Line, SHPX,* and *Railway Express Line.*

From there, my interests in advertising imagery grew to include Coca-Cola, International Harvester, John Deere, Gulf Oil, Shell, Sinclair and countless others. Logos became my thing. Knowing them, recognizing their significance and/or design. All of this started with the railroad.

My friends, cousins and I did some pretty crazy things when it came to trains. Just west and directly across from our home was a double track or switch track. Trains would crawl along the tracks and position themselves just right so another train going in the opposite direction could pass. Such was the case on one particular weekday in 1961.

Countless were the times when my bud David Smith and I would meet up after school at his house or mine for some mindless play: trading comic books, wrestling, playing basketball or "catch." We entertained one another often.

Daddy had a rule: be home sharply at 5:00 PM for dinner, no matter what. He'd often remind us, "Your mother has worked hard all day at raising you, and preparing dinner. The least you can do is be at the table when it's served."

Otherwise, we'd surely suffer the consequences. Daddy was a carpenter, working the many jobs afforded him during Atlanta's expansion years. He worked hard. I know this because on rare occasions during the summer I would go with him and spend the day watching him toil. Yes, toil. I learned the word by observing him.

Every time I hear the bluegrass song, *"Grandpa was a Carpenter," by John Prine*, I think of Daddy.

> *Grandpa wore his suit to dinner*
> *Nearly every day*
> *No particular reason*
> *He just dressed that way.*
>
> *Brown necktie and matching vest,*
> *Both his wingtip shoes*
> *He built a closet on our back porch*
> *And put a penny in a burned-out fuse.*
>
> *Chorus....*
> *Grandpa was a carpenter,*
> *He built houses, stores and banks.*
> *Chain smoked Camel cigarettes.*
> *Hammered nails in planks.*
>
> *He was level on the level,*
> *And shaved even every door,*
> *And voted for Eisenhower*
> *'cause Lincoln won the war.*
>
> *Well, he used to sing me "Blood on the Saddle"*
> *And rock me on his knee*
> *And let me listen to the radio*
> *Before we got T.V.*
>
> *He'd drive to church on Sunday*
> *And take me with him too*
> *Stained glass in every window*
> *Hearing aids in every pew.*

Now Grandma was a teacher
She went to school in Bowling Green
Traded in a milking cow
For a Singer sewing machine.

Well, she called her husband "Mister"
And walked real tall and proud
And used to buy me comic books
After Grandpa died.

> *Grandpa Was a Carpenter lyrics by John Prine*
> *copyright Warner/Chappell Music, Inc.*

Except for the "suit to dinner" and "voted for Eisenhower," this so describes Daddy. (He would never have voted for a Republican. Not in the 50's and 60's. Perhaps today though). The verse about Grandma is pretty close to describing Mama too. Some time around the late 1940s, she traded several chickens and $15.00 for her beloved Singer sewing machine. The cabinetry to the machine now serves as our sink in our home's powder room. (I wonder if she'd mind?)

At day's end, he would drag himself up the back steps, attempting to reach the back porch and the meal waiting in the kitchen. His strides were long and deliberate. Heavy. Flat-footed. Marching through the back porch and opening the door to the kitchen meant a greeting from one of his children. My ritual was to grab one of his legs, then his lunchbox to see what prize he might have left: one or two peanut butter crackers, a cookie or two. Whatever was there became mine! Riding his leg around the tiny kitchen table, to observe him planting a kiss on Mom was like a circus ride, only free. Staring upward past his lean and tired body, I would watch him plant a long, smooch kiss on the side of Mother's cheek. Something I do today. The art of "smooching" was a Brooks trait. Just lean in, pucker up, lips against cheek and plant five or six mini-kisses on a soft cheek. He didn't know it, but he taught me lots about how to love, and how to honor your wife.

After washing up, in an attempt to release the odors of the day, he would sit at the head of the table. After the tea-stirring ritual, and the irregular prayer, depending on the mood, there would be no further waiting. Everyone better be at their place. It was suppertime. His bride had worked hard at making it good and special, and by George, we should honor that by being at the table and ready to eat everything placed before us, on time. It was 5:00 PM. It was time to sup.

This particular day, I let time slip up on me. David and I were heavily into a wrestling match on the lawn of his front yard. I was always the wrestler Chief Don Eagle and he was Ray Gunkel. Our play was harmless, yet competitive and imaginative.

It was 5:05. I rose up from a certain pin move, and the sudden realization that I would be late for dinner came over me. I ran into David's house, "Miss Smith, Miss Smith, can you tell me what time it is?"

"It's about ten after, hon. You better rush home," she said.

I was never, ever late for supper. It was one of my primal fears. I ran out of the house, through the carport. Grabbing my ball cap, I rushed across the yard, giving David a cursory wave and I was off to the races. The Smith home was only about one-half mile away, separated by a manufacturing plant, two or three houses and of course, the railroad tracks.

As bad luck would have it on this particular day, a train had stopped along the tracks, awaiting a switchover and preventing me from reaching my destination. Oh my God! A Brooks child would be late for dinner. All hell might break loose. Reaching the train tracks, I attempted to peer between cars and wheels to see if Dad had made it home yet. I squinted through the freight cars, looking for his new Chevy pickup – hard to miss since it was bright red. Unfortunately there was just too much greenery for me to make anything out. Curse those boxwoods and Crape Myrtles! I worked my way westward along the tracks, trying my best to make anything out. Far too much "stuff" that Mom had so faithfully planted around our house.

I waited. And waited. The train just sat there. I was riddled with anxiety. Fearful of what may happen to me, or at least to my backside, if this blasted train didn't move itself! But soon!

I leaned forward looking eastward toward Carl, hoping to spy a caboose and determine my chances of running alongside the tracks, crossing somewhere behind it, and back down the tracks toward home. Then westward, hoping for the sight of the engines and another safe place to cross. There was nothing to see either way but train. What a quandary.

I waited still longer. Still no movement from that blasted train.

It was at least 5:20 now. My imagination ran wild. All the food would be on the table by now. Daddy would be standing at the top of the back steps with a pistol and whip, ready to let me have it as I approached. Aunt Ruby and Mama would be just behind him, making that angry face they were capable of, leaning to either side of Daddy, both curious and vengeful as to what was about to take place. Jack, of course would be in the kitchen, finishing up his meal, laughing at the prospects of my punishment, and finishing off both his and my chocolate cake. I would be flogged publicly, then shot at least ten times, hung by the neck, then the mother of all punishments, made to go to bed without my supper.

5:25 now. Life was over. I would have to run away and make a whole new life for myself. Anything to keep from facing the wrath of Daddy.

I took a quick glance under and between the cars again. I tried to imagine myself crawling under one of the train cars. I then thought about climbing between cars either over or under the coupler. "Which of these would be the least dangerous?" I asked myself. "Or was this really stupid to even think about?"

5:30. I had never been this late for dinner in my life. In fact, I had never been late, period.

It was decision time. Over the coupler. That was what I would do. I stood just aside the train cars, listening intently east and west for the sound of impending movement. Silence. I tried to think about how long it should take me to slip past the train. Then I thought of what I was to do if it began to move while I was making MY move. My heart raced. My head spun. I took one final look and leapt into action.

Running up to the coupler, I stopped and held on. The heat and hardness of the steel was foreign to me. I could feel my heart pounding in my chest. Instantly, from the touch, there was grime and grease and dirt covering my palms. The grime was an afterthought. I froze. Paralyzed from fear and utter amazement that I had placed myself in such danger. I climbed up atop the greasy coupler and balanced myself. A foreign and crippling feeling came over me. From far away, I could hear the train begin to reset itself, coupler after coupler, like dominoes. The noise was becoming closer. I realized that it would soon be right on me, and that the locomotive would be pulling the entire caravan of rail cars along, with me as its involuntary passenger. I might wind up somewhere in Waco, Texas or Abilene, Kansas, or some other God-forsaken place, before it stopped and let me off!

With another step to the opposite side of the coupler, I literally threw myself toward the south side of the tracks. Landing in sand, weeds and gravel, my feet jarred against the sweet earth and I somersaulted twice into a swollen bed of briers. I didn't care about the scratches and stings; I was alive. I could breathe again. What had I just done? Risked my life in order to avoid trouble at home?

I was alive. I had been spared.

I sat up with my arms on my knees, fingers interwoven, my back facing home, staring at the giant train that now began to slowly move, austere and cold. It seemed to be a stalking tiger, wishing it could leap from its cage-tracks and attack. Staring at the wheels that would surely have crushed little old me, their tops being my height, I jumped to my feet, brushed myself off, and raced across the highway toward home, anticipating the worse. Up the back steps, swinging open the screen door and through the porch.

I didn't even realize Daddy's truck was not there. All this for nothing?

"Where's Daddy?" I asked. Mother and Aunt Ruby were sitting at their places. Jack must have been in our room. "I guess he had to work late." Mama replied. "Where have you been?" If Daddy wasn't home, 5:00 PM at the table was much less a big deal. I think she avoided his anger as much as we did. "Sorry. The time slipped up on me."

"You've been at the Smith's house, right? Please tell me you didn't just do what I'm thinking." staring out the kitchen window at the slow-moving train headed west. It's grumbling and growling sound slowly dissipating.

"Huh? Did what? What are you talking about?" I said sheepishly.

"The train's been stopped out front for the last forty-five minutes! How did you get across?" Mama was almost hesitant to ask, being afraid of the answer.

"I walked up toward Carl and crossed behind the train." I lied. "That's why I'm late. Sorry, Mama."

It was over. I had lived through a train crossing, the hard way. Lived to tell and re-tell.

And if my children or grandchildren read this, and if they ever do such a stupid thing as this, all kinds of hell would await them.

I am my father's son after all.

~ 7 ~
Sweat and Baseball

The summer of 1967 was hot. Duh. So what else was new? It was always hot in north Georgia. We had no air conditioner, and up until my sophomore year of high school, no central heat. Still today, every time I enter a theatre or grocery store, I return to those hot summer days growing up. For those two places were the only air conditioning I ever enjoyed during my early, growing up years.

The first year of indoor plumbing, inclusive of a flushing toilet, was just after my 5th birthday. And, God forbid, Dad ever purchase a car with air conditioning! Just after our toilet was installed, I remember standing around the thing with Mom, Dad, Aunt Ruby, Jack and Karen to witness the "first flush." With twelve big eyes, we watched with amazement as the water swirled around the bowl, with its guttural sound as it disappeared down the hole. If we had been a "drinking" family, we would have popped open the champagne.

We had arrived.

Besides the luxury of a flush toilet, my parents never purchased a car with A/C or a self-propelled lawnmower until my brother and I left home. Darn it!

As already stated, Jack and I shared a bedroom, a double bed with spindle-corner posts and scribed lines in the headboard. Mother had antiqued it red and black. Yes, we were a Georgia

Bulldog family even then. The mattress sunk in the middle, thus causing one of us to constantly roll in that general direction. I still remember the pools of sweat that would gather under me on those nights the temperature barely got below 90 degrees. A large window fan would blow the hot air from the front porch over our soaked little bodies. Our pillows would smell of body odor, due to the heat and sweat. We each had distinct smells, so I knew right away, each evening, whether or not Jack had my pillow.

Years later, after going off to the Air Force and returning home on leave, Jack again took his place on the bed, him well over 6 feet and me pushing that size. The next morning over breakfast, I was quick to share with Mother, "Mom, we are too dad-gum big to be sleeping together in a double bed." That night, and every night thereafter when he was home, I slept on the sofa in the living room – a scratchy old wool thing that left me itching, but at least I wasn't butt-to-butt with another adult male.

One of my standard lines today comes from Lewis Gizzard: "I come from a large (Southern Baptist) family. In fact I never slept alone 'til I was married."

Summers at our home in Carl were probably typical of any other lower-middle class home. Of course, we didn't know we were lower-middle class. Dad had a steady job, as a carpenter, for the most part in Atlanta, some 40-50 miles away. Mother was a homemaker. Her number one job was to cook, clean the house and take care of the children. The only part-time job she ever had was as a substitute teacher at Auburn Elementary. Looking back now, it amazes me to think of all she did for us. She was truly an amazing woman.

Coining a remark made by Abraham Lincoln, "Most of who I am today, I owe to my mother."

Sweat was part of our existence. We sweated while watching TV, eating, playing and sleeping. Sweating was so much a part of our make up, I rarely gave it any serious thought. We learned to live with it. "Cut the grass, before it gets too hot!" was a constant cry of our mother's on those days, usually Fridays, that my brother and I shared that chore. A rare vacation to the mountains, or Savannah, always had its start at about 2:00 a.m., so that we would be comfortable in the car – before it "got too hot."

I remember mother cooking in the kitchen. She canned and often used a pressure-cooker. Walking through the kitchen meant steam leaping from the stove pots, with smells that filled my brain with thoughts of apples, potatoes, green beans, black-eyed peas, and the like. It's from those days that I still consider dishes like vegetable soup and Irish stew "comfort food." Mother would be wearing her comfy, baggy shorts, house shoes and a sleeveless blouse. Her apron would be laced in back, with all kinds of foods and ingredients smeared across its front. Sweat would be running down both sides of those rosy cheeks, and she would wipe her brow with that apron and just keep on cooking. She would complain about the heat, often fanning herself with a dishcloth. As a small boy, I would remember holding on to those apron strings or clutching to her leg like she was the most important person in the world. For indeed, she was. Her respite from the hot kitchen was usually a short walk to the family room, to sit down on her green vinyl armless chair by the sewing machine and watch *Mike Douglas, Phil Donohue* or *Marv Griffin*. I think she carried on a secret love affair with them.

Mother was never seen sitting in Daddy's recliner, also vinyl, even though he was away from home most every day. It was like, "That is Daddy's chair. And it's never to be sat in, except by him." If we were sitting in his recliner and Daddy entered the room, she quickly would give us one of her looks and say, "Get up! That's Daddy's chair!" Which we would, without question.

Except for the time when my oldest sister was sick, ravaged from brain cancer, and later passing, (referenced in the chapter, "Sad Times") I can never remember my mother being unhappy. It took very little to satisfy her contentment level.

We were well into June of '67, and I was approaching sixteen, about to experience my last summer of baseball with our community team. I absolutely loved playing baseball, especially as the catcher. Catching had become my main interest while watching local hero Skippy Porter play the position some six years earlier. My baseball heroes were always catchers: Yogi Berra, Elton Howard, John Roseboro, Earl Battey, Randy Hundley and Del Crandall. I even enjoyed watching the comical Choo-Choo Coleman with the bumbling Mets of that era. I loved being involved in every pitch. Calling every pitch. Making the decision as to what pitch would be thrown next. And sometimes, setting up special steal or pick-off plays.

In earlier years, my brother pitched on our team, and I would be his faithful catcher. I loved catching for him, because he had a wicked curve, with a fastball that would heat up my palm. Even a folded handkerchief strategically placed in my glove couldn't stop the blistering pain from catching one of his heaters. Most times though, the pain would quickly give way to the satisfaction of another well-placed strike, or better yet, a swinging strike out. There were plenty of those.

It was the spring of that year that I saved enough money to buy a real catcher's mitt. Larry's Easy Pay Tire Store in Winder, had a Del Crandall model that I coveted. Larry's was about the only place in Barrow County that sold baseball equipment. I would spend a typical Saturday morning with my Mother, driving to Winder, listening to her complain about the parking, then stroll over to Larry's to hold THE glove and pound it a few times. I'd inspect the price tag to see if it had changed, and wish for the way to make her mine. It was $9.95, which in that day, was a huge amount of money. It was after several grass cuttings, at $2.00 a cut ($1 from Mama and $1 from Aunt Ruby), that I finally saved up enough to buy it.

I remember that Saturday like it was yesterday. I ran full tilt from our Broad Street parking spot, two blocks east on Candler Street and through the door of Larry's. Past the counter, a quick right to sporting goods, then left down the aisle. And there it was. The glove was still there! Thank God. My McGregor Model 9280, Del Crandall Autographed catcher's mitt. It was superbly stitched, with a perfect pocket. I brought it home and each night carefully placed a baseball in the pocket, wrapping it with a belt, hoping to develop an even better pocket. On our community teams, most boys who played catcher, including me, simply used their fielder's glove. Here I was. With the real thing!

Practicing together at home always meant Jack would pitch and I would catch. I'd pace off the proper distance, and place our "plywood" home plate down at the exact spot. Jack and I fashioned out a home plate, using Dad's jigsaw and some 4-ply plywood. The mound was a small mound of topsoil near the fig bush that grew atop our septic tank. Those figs were always the best. I'm just happy now that I didn't know then, why. Home plate was situated next to Mama's clothesline. After Daddy built the clothesline, complete with stretched vinyl-wrapped wire and cemented pipe T-bars, Mama said she was, "Happier than if it had been a new electric dryer."

That old home plate would last us several years, before finally giving way to the weather. With no gear on, and one of Jack's fastballs skipping the ground, this usually meant lots of time searching through the weeds and briars, after my "miss-catch." And, if we couldn't find it, we would fetch a hard-rubber ball and continue our session together. Oftentimes, weeks or even years would go by before we would find the elusive sphere – most often waterlogged from seasons of rain and snow, but usable nonetheless. A waterlogged ball was better than no ball at all. Besides, after hitting or throwing it against the wall a few times, and its missing cover, some electric tape wrapped around the ball would return it to its original weight, or so we thought.

Except for basketball in the fall and winter, and some one-on-one tackle football in the side yard between our and Aunt Ruby's house, baseball was king.

Jack having "aged-out" of community ball, Mike Corley was our new pitcher that summer. He and I had known each other for years, but it was that summer that we became close friends. Mike had the easiest delivery I had ever seen. Yet the ball would fly into my glove with surprising accuracy and speed. Mike had a good breaking ball, knuckle ball and even a pretty good screwball. After school, we would meet at his house and map out our strategy for the upcoming season. Thinking that other teams would be stealing our signs (comical now), we devised finger signs: 1-2-3 for a fastball, 2-3-1 for a curve, and 3-2-1 for a screwball. Four fingers was a knuckleball and a fist was a pitchout. We were like Whitey Ford and Yogi Berra, making plans for multiple strikeouts and ground balls. Our world revolved around our abilities to "play ball." We were IN our element.

I would literally pray on game day for the many clouds in the air to please not turn black. The worst thing in the world was a rainout. Our games were few and far-between, and the risk of not making up a rainout was too much to even think about. Heat was what we wanted. Hot, dry days when sweating was an incredibly satisfying thing, nothing like the sweat from a 95-degrees, sleepless night, or strolling through Mom's kitchen.

The season began with us meeting at a little league field in Winder, for our first practice session. Childhood best friend and left fielder David Smith was there, along with my cousin Mark Hayman and several others who made up our team. Butch Lance was our first baseman. Butch was a huge guy, who would become All-Region in football at Winder-Barrow High School. He could hit a ball a country mile, but it would take him an eternity to round the bases. Butch had been our catcher in years past, but our now-outdated catcher's equipment wouldn't fit him. I, on the other hand, was so skinny, the chest protector could slide right on and off without the nuisance of buckling/unbuckling most players required.

Mr. Norman Kurts agreed to be our Coach. His experience as an old barnstorming fast pitch softball pitcher lent itself well to coaching – though his "coaching" usually meant hitting a few ground balls and watching us play. None of that really mattered. He was our coach, and we had to have someone to lead us and most importantly, make up our schedule. Most of us settled on our own positions. His first question to us was "Who plays where?"

I knew exactly where I belonged: my beloved spot behind home plate.

As that first practice session wound down, I was about as content as a 15-year-old can be. I knew I was going to be the starting catcher, and before leaving, I even managed to hint at wishing to be the leadoff hitter when our season began. Who ever heard of a catcher hitting leadoff? I didn't care; I wanted that first at-bat.

Mike and I practiced practically every day. Often, David or Mark would fill in as the hitter. With no equipment on my skinny frame, they weren't allowed to swing, but they provided a great natural look to whom Mike could throw, and for me to catch. We practiced our signals and prepared ourselves for *THE* season, the one I knew would be my last (16-year-olds were too old).

We would have team practices once or twice a week, or whenever Coach Kurts could get home in time. We hungered for the experience of practicing and playing ball. Knowing that I had practice that evening usually meant a mental day off at school. Nothing else really mattered. Just Ball.

Our first game came against Union Baptist in the Holsenbeck school area near Winder. They were a pretty strong team with two good pitchers. I would later become friends with one of them – Dennis Griffin. Dennis was a short, stocky kid with a springboard delivery, and hard to hit. We would play them to a 6-6 tie, when the rains came.

I still remember being ahead of them 6-3, earlier in the game, when they had two men on base. We were well through four or five innings, with seven scheduled to play. Their best hitter, a tall, rangy kid named Kenny Ross who played 1st base for them, came to bat. He batted left, and had already had a run-scoring double that day, with Mike striking him out with a knuckleball his second time up.

His third time at bat, we started him out with a fastball, our usual strategy. Ball, outside. Another fastball was fouled away. Knowing that this kid liked pitches up, I ordered up a curve, hoping Mike could keep it low. It bounded into the dirt and got by me, with both runners advancing. I always felt it okay to call up most any pitch from Mike, as long as he had less than 3 balls on the hitter. Mike had a wicked knuckleball that he had been working on that summer, so here it would come, in spite of the fact he sometimes could be a bit wild with it. The hitter took a vicious swing, his batting helmet flying off his head, twisting into the ground, explaining "Good Grief!" as the ball popped into my mitt. No sweeter sound existed to this catcher than a swinging strike settling into the soft leather sweet spot of my "Del Crandall."

Two-and-two now. It was getting late in the game, and I knew we probably wouldn't have to face this guy again. I could see the clouds growing dark beyond the right field honeysuckles and train tracks. The steeple of Carl Baptist Church glowed bright white, as a fitting forefront to the ominous clouds behind. The skies were going to open any minute. I called time and went to the mound. When meeting on the mound, Mike and I would always go ahead and call the next pitch, then, I would go through an array of signals, all meaning nothing. "All right, come on. Let's get this guy. What do you think? How about a screwball?" Mike had been working on a screwball a lot that summer, specifically for left-handed hitters. The problem was when it didn't break, it became a pitch perfectly set up for the hitter. We sure didn't want that.

"OK." Mike said, trusting that I knew what I was doing. I settled into my crouch and went through my meaningless signals. A quick look at the runner at third, then at second. Mike's windup, and the pitch. Man! Did that pitch break! Ross swung, purely in a protective mode, just getting a piece of it, as it bounded off my facemask. "Clang!" went the mask, and my brain. A little stunned, I rose, shaking off the cobwebs. What Mike had just thrown was one of the best screwballs I had ever seen, and this kid had stayed alive with it.

What was a catcher to do but order up another one. I was 100% confident Ross couldn't hit a screwball that well-pitched, twice in a row. So here it came – another 3-2-1 call for another screwball. Mike shook it off. Apparently, he didn't want to push his luck. I had not considered it luck. I gave it to him again, so he gave way to my "wisdom." His comfortable stretch move followed by the ball headed for the sweet confines of my glove. Unfortunately, it never reached it. The crack of the bat was unlike anything I had heard before. I gazed skyward toward right field and knew right away. *Everyone* knew it was gone, but just how far? The ball sailed high and deep, far beyond the honeysuckles, bounding off the gravel of the railroad tracks. Home run. 6-6. I had asked for Mike's second screwball in a row, and it was something akin to what he and I would throw to one another while warming up. No break at all. Sort of like a slow fastball perfectly thrown over the high-middle part of the plate, and then perfectly hit off a yellow-pine, 32-ounce Lousville Slugger.

I stood, tilted my facemask atop my head and watched in amazement, feeling suddenly sick to my stomach, and very much responsible for insisting Mike throw a pitch the hitter had just seen. I was at fault. I had been waiting and working, insisting this day come, and it had. A day to play ball. And win, dog gone it!

Their players came out to greet him at home plate. I stepped aside and watched. Disappointed. Sullen. I started to join them. After all, I was as much responsible for his homer as he was. Why weren't they slapping *ME* on the back?

We had practically won the game. Butch had hit a homer. I had a triple and a couple of stolen bases and even scored twice. Mike and David had had great days at the plate too. All for naught, because with one little pitch, one screwball too many, and the win was washed away.

It wasn't another half-inning that the game itself was washed away too. I still remember the feeling of helplessness as I boarded my Dad's red Chevy truck, glove and bat in hand, wet from the now-torrential thunderhead. But no tears. Mom's comment was, "At least you didn't lose." Somehow, I didn't feel that way at all. We had lost, to my way of thinking. And yet, still no tears.

After all, for a day, I had done nothing but play ball. Been a participant in a ritual older than my deceased grandfather. Stood behind the plate and made every decision as to what pitch to throw next. Felt the sweat of the padding of my catcher's mask slipping across my face. Sensed the tickling droplets of moisture on my back running down my soiled T-shirt. Enjoyed another day off from school, chores and homework - a love affair I had with a game.

I had sweated...and I had played ball.

Jack & Me, 1958.
A buzz-cut every two weeks,
whether we needed it or not.

~ 8 ~
Please Don't Call My Name

Another year came and went. Time seemed so slow back then. One school grade became another. I watched as friendships changed and siblings grew older. It was 1966. I was in my tenth grade year at a school where I was just a name. Small for my age. The perfect target for bullying. (Oh, could I list a few names here!) Acne. High-pants. Glasses. A regular Napoleon Dynamite, only shorter.

Afraid of my own shadow, I was miserable during my high school years. Well, at least most of them. They were filled with the constant battle of trying to fit in. Who would I sit with on the bus? Who would I hang with during lunch? What classes would I take? What clubs would I join? Would I ever be as successful and popular as my brother and sisters? Will I still have the same friends? Can I get with the "Winder crowd?" Or should I, even?

I also worried about my studies and my grades, although I was very average at best. I longed for a time like my elementary school years, when all-A's could be earned with very little effort. Hardly any studying at all. I longed for my Auburn Elementary and its small intimate surrounding, where I could be somebody. Play ball again. Be on a team. Have lots of friends. Fewer responsibilities. No cares.

Auburn Elementary, for grades one through eight, was my sanctuary. I had always felt like somebody there. Aunt Ruby had been my first-grade teacher. Miss Rainey and Miss House had taught me in my second-through-fourth grade years. And Mom would often be at the school, performing substitute-teaching duties. These women had all been mothers to me. I always was made to feel special, though I'm certain now, I was not. Aunt Ruby pushed me toward a love for drawing and painting and being creative. My Mother pushed me toward excelling in schoolwork; I received my first 'non-A' in 7th grade. And my brother pushed me in sports, creating in me a special affinity for basketball and baseball.

Jack and I were a competitive pair. Everything from football and basketball, to ping-pong and Rook. We were at each other a lot, trying to prove ourselves superior. Little did he know he was instilling in me a competitive spirit that would come in handy, in so many ways, later in life.

The school at Auburn had been my bastion. A sleepy, little school and town some five miles from Winder. Auburn sat immediately west of Carl, both little hamlets in western Barrow County, about 50 miles east of Atlanta and 35 miles from Athens, Georgia. Auburn Elementary served all White families in the Auburn/Carl/Harbins (western) areas of Barrow County. African-American children throughout the 163-square-mile county attended the only school available to them at that time: Glenwood, closed to desegregation in 1970.

Auburn had one long hallway with eight classrooms. Lower-aged children had bathrooms that were connected to two rooms each. Every room was floored with slick concrete and walled with cement blocks. Though institutional in so many ways, we grew to love the old place. It was home for us every day, September to May. Halloween carnivals, doughnut sales, rummage sales. Whatever we could do to make money was how the school grew and evolved.

My Mother had been the PTA President my 5th grade year at Auburn. Miss Pared was my teacher. It was evident to me early on, that she didn't really enjoy teaching. She was very stern, rarely smiled, and seemed to despise children. I did whatever was necessary to stay in her good graces. The thing I best remember learning from Miss Pared was my "states-and-capitals." To this day, I still know them, though as they say, "That and a quarter might get you a cup of coffee." I learned from her, mostly out of fear, however.

It was in that year that I experienced my first time as part of a "team." As stated, I had played community baseball at the community field near our church (and cemetery), and had played as much as I could with some of the older boys during recess, whenever a teacher would formulate teams.

Mr. Fortner was the school's Seventh grade teacher, and coached most every sport at the school. We had no gym at the time, so basketball games were played on a dirt court, lined by a stick-bearing, steady hand. Only Winder, Statham, Holsenbeck and Bethlehem had gyms during those days. Our baseball field was a long walk behind the school, where stood a rickety backstop with plenty of holes, some patched, but most gaping. I had spent my share of time on that field playing with the boys from grades Six through Eight, seemingly much older than me. I was friends with several of the Sixth graders too: Tom Clark, Butch Lance and Ronnie Gilkrease, but several of the other Seventh and Eighth-graders were not only too old for me, but too big as well, and thus bullies. Older brother Jack was in the eighth-grade that year. He was small for his age, as was I. Both of us tolerated our fair-share of bullying from boys bigger, and as I discovered later, not so bright. Many of these bullies had been passed on each year as "social promotion." To my dismay, when they had *not* passed, they became closer and closer to my school grade. Growing up in Carl and Auburn, bullying was a big problem for my brother and me. I suppose in hindsight, the community was readying us for what would be our plight in high school. Until we both hit growth-spurts late in high school, we often found ourselves easy targets for bullies. In our little eyes, there were plenty of them, too.

Our school had a roughshod baseball team that year. Jack played, along with Ronnie Evert, Roger Knowles, and others. I played, if only to get along. I had no aspirations of playing at their level. I was basically killing recess time, and trying to avoid the bullies.

A day arrived late in the year when our school team had a baseball game scheduled with Bethlehem Elementary at their school's field. I was vaguely aware of the game and somewhat enthusiastic about our schools' playing one another, but never dreamed of actually participating. Never as a fifth-grader.

It was mid-day, having just completed lunch, and we were sitting down to a history session. I could hear the hustle-and-bustle of students who were prepping to be transported to Bethlehem for the big game, of little concern to me. Suddenly, Mr. Fortner appeared, stepping through the open doorway of our classroom: "Excuse me, Miss Pared, but could you excuse David Brooks and Mike Corley for our game today?"

My heart sank. Suddenly, nerves ran rampant through my little four-foot frame. I had visions of me coming to bat with runners at second and third, two outs in the last inning, and us down by one run. The future of the civilized world was thrust on my shoulders. I slowly got up from my desk and followed Mike to the door, wishing with all my heart that the man had called someone else's name.

"Get your gloves, boys. You're going with us to Bethlehem for the game today," he said. The words echoed through my skull. I couldn't believe it. Little old Fifth grader, blue-jean wearing, cow-licked head, knock-kneed me! I was going to go to the game? As a member of the team? Was old man Fortner completely out of his mind?

Chills ran up my spine. I shuttered. Aunt Ruby would say, "A rabbit just ran over your grave." On that day, I was wishing I was *in* that grave. Maybe I could tell him I was sick. Or that I had to go home and attend a funeral. Mine!

The ride to Bethlehem was only about fifteen minutes. It seemed a lot longer. Mike and I sat together. "Do you think we'll play?" he asked. I didn't answer; I just stared out the window and prayed to God that we wouldn't. I was still in shock. Completely transfixed on what could be. What I hoped *wouldn't* be.

As it turned out, we were both put in the game in the bottom of the last inning, with a two-run lead, to play defense. As I trotted out to left field, Roger Knowles, our pitcher said to Mike and me, "Don't screw up this lead, kid."

I reached my position and turned to face the infield. I gazed over to center field and spotted Mike. Then I began praying. On every pitch. "Please God, don't let a ball be hit my way. Please!" I remember the clouds spinning overhead. I remember mouthing these words over and over, " I will not throw up. I will not throw up. I will not throw up."

First batter up, a strikeout. "Whew! Thank you God." I said to no one in particular. Second batter, a base hit to right field. Then a walk and a wild pitch. Runners at Second and Third now with only one out. Coach Fortner came to the mound. "Could this inning ever end?" I questioned.

The next hitter took Roger deep into the count when he hit a screaming liner right over the third baseman, bouncing toward my right. Trying my best to focus, I somehow backhanded the ball, preventing it from going into the corner. Surprised at the realization that the ball was in my glove, I clumsily turned and threw it back in to the shortstop as quickly as I could. To my amazement, the runner at second had held up. He had not scored on the play! We still had the lead!

I was so thrilled at my play, I barely remember the next two outs, but I do recall the last pitch from Roger to the Bethlehem hitter – a popup to second base. I can still see the players' excitement over that last-pitch out and our victory. I remember my excitement too – not over the last pitch. Not over the victory. But over the fact that I actually had played in a game with eighth graders and had not made a complete fool of myself, for most assuredly I would have, had that ball made its way into the left field corner. Thank God I never went to bat!

I had survived. I had not passed out. And I had not thrown up. Please God, don't ever let me hear my name called out like that again. Please!

I had been through the valley of the shadow of death on that little diamond in Bethlehem, Georgia, and had lived to tell the story. The story of a little boy who loved to play ball.

But, on this day, wanted no part of it.

~ 9 ~
Cousins

The Brooks family was a big community. Like me, Daddy was the sixth child in his family. Only he and his siblings numbered nine, one dying in infancy. All of William Allen and Anna Lee Parker Brooks's children did okay, including Joe. That is to mean, they stayed out of prison, raised decent children and managed to provide for their families. All of them must have thought that being part of a big family was "just what you did." (Must have been a lot of cold, cold nights under those covers, for the Brookes.)

Mom, on the other hand was the oldest of only two, her only sibling being a half-sister. She never knew her father, as he died when Mom was only nine months old. Though she was close to her mother, Mom quickly grew up, being raised by her maternal grandparents, the Millers, in the small community of Campton. After high school at Monroe, where she was the Salutatorian, she married and was soon raising children. All of my cousins on Mother's side were the children of my Aunt Polly, Mom's sister. Aunt Polly moved to California with Granny as a young girl, when Granny decided, "There's just too many kids around for me." She of course was referring to all the children being born from Mom and Dad. Being all the way across the world from California, and able to do very little traveling, we never were very close to the Rekow cousins. They were at most distant acquaintances. Sort of makes me sad today, but happily through the wonders of Facebook, I'm able to maintain a semblance of kinship with them.

A distance problem was never so evident with my Brooks cousins. They were everywhere but fairly local – from Midvale (in Burke County, Georgia) to Atlanta, cousins were a constant for me. We six children of Joe and Nina had nineteen 1st cousins and fifty-five second cousins, the latter being more my age.

Hours and hours of play and fun were spent with the Hayman children, offspring of Margaret and Otis Hayman. Margaret was the child of Lottie Brooks Miller, Daddy's sister, and was the first-born grandchild of his parents. Being twenty-plus years my senior, I always thought of her more as an aunt, instead of a cousin. Her children were more my generation, and the Haymows and we lived very close to one another. Otis and Dad were both carpenters and worked together for years sharing rides to and from the various job sites in and around Atlanta.

Their only son, Mark, was three years younger than me, and we became close cousins. We walked the tracks together, made kudzu tunnel towns, climbed trees high enough to see far-off Stone Mountain, fished the lakes and ponds of Barrow County, and sneaked a smoke or two, now and then.

Our mischief was harmless, and we "adventured" around like escaped convicts, only not looking for trouble.

Camping was a big deal. Besides the many trips with Otis and Margaret, our parents' best friends, camping at Rock Creek or Tallulah River, Mark and I enjoyed camping all to ourselves far behind the Church Cemetery, deep in the backwoods. Another cousin, Butch Miller, would often join us. (Butch now serves as a state Senator for the Gainesville area.)

We could easily walk to our "camping sweet spot" and feel like we were far away from civilization, so as to be ourselves. Our campsite was a small clearing among hundreds of medium-sized pines. It was the perfect location for a nice campfire, hot dogs, Vienna sausages, potato chips and lots of gossip into the wee hours of the night. Plenty of straw too, lay all around, making for great fire starter. It's no small wonder that we didn't burn down all of western Barrow County. This "sweet spot" also provided a perfect opening through the trees, just big enough for stargazing

We'd often fish at night in the lake owned by the Haymows and nearby our golden campsite. Frog gigging was a favorite pastime. We'd spy them with a flashlight and make a quick stab at their glowing eyes. If ever we were quick enough to spear one, we'd brag on its size and marvel at its muscular legs and torso. But, we never ate them; animal activists would not have approved.

One night while lying in our sleeping bags and doing some serious night-sky gazing, we heard something we had never heard before.

Earlier that night, we had talked about escaped convicts, murderers, and other hoodlums, all of whom were nowhere near Barrow County. This was not long after a crazy named Richard Speck had broken into a nursing school dorm in Chicago and had systematically killed several of the young ladies. Like all curious boys, this was intriguing, but most of all, sad and sick. We spoke in detail of what we had read. The stories chilled us. We were ripe for a night of fright.

The sound echoed through the still night. Neither of us could identify the noise. Was it an animal? Or human? Mark and I both froze. Butch's bulging eyes glowed in the flickering campfire. I could hear them both slowly pulling up the covers of their sleeping bags. I began to do the same.

We were miles from anyone's homes. No place of safety could possibly save us from whatever lurked deep within those woods.

The noise almost sounded like a screaming baby. "What the hell was that?" Mark asked. Though we were pretty innocent in so many ways, we could both let off a good four-letter word, now and then. "I don't know! What does it sound like?" "It sounds to me like somebody is killing a baby." Wild and gory images must have swum around in our heads. I had visions of Richard Speck, stomping through the pines in search of three little boys who had done some bad things in their lives, and deserved the worse. Bad things like smoking rabbit tobacco, coming home late for supper and laying coins on the tracks. Really serious stuff. Speck was so big and crazy, he would be parting the pines, marching through the woods. Just like King Kong. Like how I had envisioned mighty Paul Bunion. Axe and all.

I pulled my covers up a little more. The fire began to die.

"Mark, get up and go get some pine straw. The fire's going out." I whispered. Though terribly smoky and smelly, the dry and ever present straw could quickly flame up, becoming a little torrent. And provide us with immediate light.

"No way, Dave. YOU go get it. I'm not going out in those woods with that thing out there!"

"Come on dude! What'aya SCARED of? Chicken!! Baca-baca-baca-baca! Come on. The fire's about to go out! Get some."

"Why don't you go get it? Huh?" Mark came back.

"I would, but I'm way too comfortable in my bag. Besides, the zipper's stuck," I lied.

"Yeah, right." He replied, with eyes rolling. I could see the whites of his eyes in the low firelight. He wasn't buying my lame excuse.

"No, really! It's caught in the bag's lining. I can't get out!" pretending to pull on the bag's side.

Suddenly another cry out by whatever the heck it was in those woods. We stopped arguing about who would get pine straw and froze in our bags again. The sound was a lot closer. Whatever or whoever was disrupting our campout was decidedly closer – like it was practically IN our campsite.

"Maybe it's Richard Speck!" said Butch. I trembled a little, pretending to be brave. I suspect he could see the whites of my eyes as well.

"Come on! What do you think? The guy escaped from Chicago, and decided to come to Carl, Georgia? What are ya' crazy?"

Another cry. Closer still. There was now no talk out of either one of us. We lay perfectly still. No wind. No nothing. No rustling leaves. No other sound. Just the low crackle of a dying fire. And the heaving heart beats of three dying, little boys. At least, we *thought* we were going to die.

Then a noise, like someone walking through the woods, almost like they were stomping out sticks and limbs, just so they could be heard. We sat up a little and stared out into the darkness. Nothing to see. Just black and bleak, total darkness. Oh my Gosh, I thought I would die right there, or at the very least, wet my pants.

We sat up on our elbows and peered out toward the direction of the noise.

"Oh shit!" cried Mark. On the rare occasions that we used that word, you knew it was serious. "Oh shit is right!" I returned. "We're goners."

The noise came closer, and louder. Each step seemed to echo through the baby pines. I started to think about my parents, all my friends, about my dogs, and how I would miss them. About my sisters and brother.

A small consolation was that I wouldn't have to take that math quiz on Monday. Then I began to pray that I COULD take that math quiz on Monday.

I detected a large figure, attempting to hide behind a pine. It was human all right, but who? We both tucked our heads deep in our sleeping bags and began to whimper, ever so slightly, so as not to be heard by the other. Big guys like us don't cry!

Then a large growl and a silhouetted figure leaped out from the pines into a clearing just in front of us. Knees bent, feet apart. Two big hands widespread, with bent fingers. Speck!

"ARRRRRR-UHHHHHHHH!" he growled.

I dared not peek. I could hear Mark's bag trembling in the sand around the fire. A drop of sweat ran down my back. I didn't care. Just, please God, let me live.

Then laughter. "HAH-HAH-HAH-HAH-HAH" together with a huge slap on a blue-jeaned knee. I quickly pulled down my bag to look out and see my brother Jack rolling in the dirt. He had gotten us good.

"You butthead! You jerk! That's not funny! You scared us to death!" we shouted.

Half hearing us, he couldn't stop laughing. I was so mad. Mark and Butch knew better than to get mad at Jack. My brother was always several inches taller than I. And, he really dwarfed those two.

Jack sat down by the fire with a big ker-thump, still laughing and slapping the dirt. Then, the "cry" went out again. Mark and I stopped berating Jack, looked at him and noted that he had no response to this wild and wooly sound. Looking out at big brother, I asked, "Do you know what that is?"

"You dummies. That's an owl. A screech owl to be exact." Him acting all knowing. We fell back in our bags with relief. We had been tortured by my big brother, only to be relieved by his answer. Richard Speck was out of our minds for the rest of that night.

We joined Jack in his laughter, half embarrassed and mostly relieved.

"He still could be a real butthead sometimes, though." I thought to myself.

Charlotte Garmin was the daughter of Geneva Brooks Garmin, the daughter of my Dad's oldest brother, Emmett and his wife Mary Ellen. Charlotte lived in neighboring Walton County on a dairy farm with her mother and grandparents. She was fifteen days older than I.

I don't recall the first time we played together and became close, but I'm certain it had something to do with Aunt Ruby, who would spend a week with Uncle Emmett and Aunt Mary Ellen Brooks each summer. Charlotte and I were extremely close. Our gender difference never stood in the way of our friendship. We were both raised on small farms in very rural settings. We both attended church regularly, though her immediate family was Methodists, mine Baptists. We were about the same size and basically loved a lot of the same things: mainly playing house.

Yeah, that's right, I'm not ashamed to admit it. I played house. I'd like to think that I was "secure in my masculinity." We'd do the typical thing with her as the mother, and me as the businessman father.

I loved her home in Bold Springs. There were lots of dairy cows, great climbing trees, a swing set and even a school bus and farm tractor on which to sit and pretend, though Uncle Emmett didn't approve of playing on either vehicle.

Around 1956, the Emmett Brooks clan was visiting Aunt Ruby for Sunday dinner. Charlotte and I were eating in a back room, at the "kid's table" while the adults ate at the kitchen's dining table. I thought Charlotte hung the moon. She had golden brown hair, dimples and a winsome smile. She was one of the nicest friends I ever had, in that she took a genuine interest in me, and I in her.

We were munching away on some of Aunt Ruby's fried chicken, with six adults chatting and eating away in the adjoining kitchen. Thinking that no one could hear us, I blurted out to Charlotte, "You're my girlfriend!" The kitchen let out with a thunderous roar, led by Uncle Emmett. He had the loudest, most recognizable laugh of any Brooks I knew. I froze, looked at Charlotte and asked, "Are they laughing at us?" Another outburst of laughter. "I think so. Actually, I think they're laughing at *you*," she said.

I shut up.

On their Bold Springs farm, Charlotte and I would sit in the small, elevated windows of the dairy barn and watch as the cows came loping into the barn. Most of them were Holsteins, though a few were Jerseys. Uncle Emmett had a name for every cow, and Charlotte knew just about all of them. What a fascination it was to watch these milk producers enter their rightful place along the milk line, readying themselves for their twice daily feeding and milking.

Uncle Emmett's son, Charles also helped with the milking. He would laugh at us as we called out the names of each cow, sometimes right, sometimes wrong. "That's Bimbo. Here comes Flossie. This one's Sophie. That one's Myrtle. And Lucy." The ritual was great fun.

On the times we couldn't recall their names, Charles would shout it out in a hurry. He knew them all.

Once as we were calling out the names, one of them let out a big poop, together with some deafening farts as well. "OOOOOOO-eeeeeeeeee, That's Nellie!" We'd cry out. Charles would quickly retort, "That's not Nellie today. That's Potpie today!" We'd laugh uncontrollably. What great and innocent days those were.

Charlotte's mother seemed more like an aunt than a first cousin. She'd bring out the sprinkler and let us run through it, on a hot summer's day. I loved the apples and pears that came from the back and side yards. A quick and convenient afternoon snack, much like our home in Carl.

Charlotte always came to Carl for Vacation Bible School at Carl Baptist Church. I loved her visits. It meant having a playmate

24-7 who would not "pick on me." This particular VBS, we made ash trays out of play-dough. Today, I can't help but chuckle over making ASH TRAYS at church. Another contribution to my mixed-up world. I wonder if a VBS teacher ever made beer-holders? Not at teetotalling Carl Baptist Church they didn't. In pure innocence, we called it "tea-toting."

One year, Charlotte and I were chosen to sing a duet at the Friday night commencement of Bible School. We practiced each day and prepared for the big event. That Friday came around, and we took our places in front of the pulpit to sing our special arrangement of "How Great Thou Art." Charlotte had on this precious white dress with patent-leather shoes. She was as pretty as Elaine Roark. Her hair was perfectly brushed, with a hair band across the back. She was a living doll, even to a klutz like me.

I wore the customary white shirt, dark pants and red bowtie. I must have looked a little like PeeWee Herman standing next to Marilyn Monroe.

The piano began with a short prelude. Then, we blurted out "Oh Lord, my God, When I in awesome wonder, consider all...." Looking out on the congregation, I wasn't sure if they were laughing at us or for us. We were the hit of the program, or so we thought. Our mothers and Aunt Ruby couldn't stop bragging on us; how well we sang and how cute we were. CUTE!??! I wanted nothing to do with cute. All I could think about was forgetting the words a time or two, and my voice cracking several times.

Have you ever seen the "Our Gang" episode when Alfalfa sings a solo to impress Darla? That was Charlotte and me. I probably had the pointed cow-lick too.

Still today, I stay in touch with Charlotte. She's Charlotte Wheeler now, with three grown children and several grandchildren. At a recent family reunion at which a bluegrass band was playing, she and I got together and very nearly got up to sing once again "How Great Thou Art." We didn't do it, but we sure had fun laughing at the prospect. Still love that girl so. All ways will.

Other cousins came and went through the old redwood farmhouse I called home. My older cousin Stanley coached me in basketball in the Eighth grade. Dolly Hayman and Janis Miller were my "Cold Duck" drinking buddies at the Lawrenceville Drive-in, where we first experimented with that marginal brew.

Bennie and Walton Brooks visited often, as they had relatives from both sides of their parents living in Barrow County. And Randy Brooks, the youngest of the twenty-five Brooks cousins came as well.

More memorable than Randy's visits were the trips we took to *his* home in Midvale, Georgia. His Dad, my Uncle Orien, was the Superintendent of the University of Georgia Experimental Station in Midvale. What a spread! I naturally thought this was HIS farm. Upon visits, Randy, Jack and I would sit on the tailgate of his old GMC pickup and drive the farm roads. Uncle Orien enjoyed stopping on occasion and picking a few prize tomatoes or ears of corn to give to Daddy. They'd laugh out loud, with remarks like, "Wouldn't old Papa kill for one of these 'maters!" Daddy loved all his brothers and sisters to death, but I think he felt a special kinship with his brother Orien. I think it was because Orien was the baby, but also because, though very successful and educated, Orien never wore those traits on his sleeve. Around Daddy, he was just one of the Brooks boys.

The Brooks cousins were numerous, boisterous, and probably obnoxious to some. But we shared a love for family, laughter and playful antics never intended to hurt anyone. From chasing fireflies on a hot July evening to sitting on the ice cream churn while Daddy cranked up a gallon of the sweet cream, or climbing to a tree's upper branches just to sway back and forth and hear Aunt Ruby call out, "You're going to break your neck!"

Thankfully, and mercifully, no one ever did.

While it's true that "You can't go home again," I'm thankful for those great memories that send me back there in my mind.

Mama & Daddy
circa 1976
in the famous black vinyl recliner

Mother and Granny
circa 1923

She loved dogs too.
circa 1923

Mother was the Salutatorian of her Senior class.
Front row, fourth from right. Monroe High School, 1935.
Joe's brother Ben, front row, third from left.

Mother and her four baby girls.
She made the dresses they're wearing.
Clockwise: Sandra (top left), Marilyn, Dorian and Karen
circa 1945

1950 in her kitchen

Joe Jack Brooks
Monroe A&M
Circa 1922

Joe (with hair!)
circa 1948

Joe with 3 of his 4 brothers
(L-R): Emmett, Rufus,
Orien & Joe
(Ben, not pictured)

Ruby Estelle Brooks
Circa 1940

Five of the six Brooks children, with Sandra supervising.
L-R: Dorian, Sandra, Jack, Marilyn, Karen - 1948

Sandra, 1954

Lawson & Sandra Brady
with children Terri & Steve
1958

Marilyn, circa 1945　　　*Marilyn, circa 1948*

8th Grade, Auburn Elementary, 1951
Marilyn is front row second from right
(Lawson Brady is the teacher, back row far right.)

Marilyn, 1954

Dorian, 1941   *Dorian, circa 1948*

Marilyn, Dorian & Sandra
1942

Winder-Barrow Homecoming Court, class of 1959
Dorian is back row third from right

Karen, 1949

Karen, 1956

Karen, 1961

Karen (middle) with her siblings.
Paris, 1989

Jack, 1948

Cowboy Jack, 1953

Jack, 1954

Jack, 1959

Jack & me, 1953

*1st Grade
Knucklehead
1956*

Mom & Dad with
Otis & Margaret Hayman
1966

Rev. Claude Healan
Cherokee, NC
circa 1955

Charlotte Garmin
1969

With Mark Hayman
Talullah River, 1966

David Smith
1963

Sister Amelda
1961

The old homeplace
just before being leveled in 2008

The only existing photo that includes all six of us. (L-R): David, Jack, Karen, Dorian, Marilyn & Sandra on the road from our Savannah vacation – 1959

1988, (L-R): Jack, Dorian (front), Karen, Marilyn & me

Carl Baptist Church (before relocation)

Auburn Elementary School

~ 10 ~
Heroes All

What would life be like for a little boy in the 1950s and 60s, if he didn't have heroes? Real and imaginary, I had plenty.

From the time I could remember, I loved cowboys. Television drove that. *Roy Rogers, Gene Autry,* and later *Sugarfoot, Wanted Dead or Alive, Maverick, Bat Masterson, Paladin, The Lone Ranger,* and on and on.

I knew what day and time each show came on. I'd plan my homework and the day's activities or chores around watching these shows. Roy and his beautiful golden-haired horse, Trigger. No one could rear his horse up and fire into the air more beautifully than Roy. Even Dale and her horse Buttermilk were favorites.

"Hey, Cisco! Hey, Poncho!" What a twosome were the Cisco Kid and Poncho! His horse, Diablo, was a favorite too – a gorgeous palomino, perfectly spotted in black and white. I yearned to have at least one of these beautiful animals. "Daddy, can we buy a horse? We already have cows, and the pasture would be perfect."

"Boy, you can't EAT a horse. It'd be just a waste of money. All they ever do is eat and poop." I couldn't understand the man. Why couldn't we have an animal that may cost hundreds in upkeep, and provide us no significant sustenance? Daddy was into only owning things that were useful. Especially food or shelter.

Daddy kept lots of wood scraps around the house. There were planks and molding and the like stacked up in the water-filled basement. A good steady rain would fill the muddy basement to where the only way you could traverse it was to step on well-placed bricks. The upper reaches of the barn were full of wood scraps too, only reachable by standing on the rusty old feed drums. There was carpentry wood stacked in the crawl space, along the side of the house, in the well house, behind the barn. You get the picture. Truth be known, Daddy probably could have built a small house with all the wood he collected. Every work site he ever jobbed had plenty of wood scraps left over from that particular project. Wood that would be burned otherwise. He would often come home with a truck full, confident that someday he would use them. And indeed a lot of it, he did.

Our family room paneling looked like the inside of the Piedmont Driving Club in Atlanta, where he had completed the finishing carpentry in its dining room and bar areas. Our bookshelves above the television mimicked display shelves at Neiman-Marcus. The kitchen was tiled similar to offices at the Atlanta Airport, and the ceiling could pass for C&S Bank offices. He'd save every little piece he could, in order to provide a comfortable home for his family. Our home was a mish-mash of walls, flooring and ceilings not unlike building and job sites all over the Atlanta area. I knew of no other kid who could brag that pieces of the Governor's Mansion might be found in any part of our house, for Dad had completed the famous and often-photographed winding staircase of the Georgia Governor's Mansion.

Though Daddy saw all of this wood as pieces HE could use to build, I saw them as play things. A 1" x 4" was a precious commodity. I could take a piece, especially if it was already painted white, cut it to a specific length, then using a black crayon, color in the spots to look just like Cisco's pony. It could provide me with hours and hours of fun. And even though my horse had no head, it didn't really matter. It was the Palomino I always wanted. Another plank already stained a gold amber would be my Trigger.

I even had a special place I would park my "horses" – in the corner of the sub-porch space just below the back steps, among

Daddy's tools. Daddy's tools were special to him. They occupied a privileged space in the corner. So should my horses.

My first bicycle was "Trigger." Mama and I were shopping in Lawrenceville one day. It was a few weeks before Christmas, and we were in the local Western Auto store, when I spied her. She was drop-dead gorgeous – white sidewall tires, training wheels, a push-button horse sound, and plastic gold-and-white buckskin fringe flowing from the ends of the handlebars. There was even a plastic satchel covering the chain's large sprocket. It was my dream-bike! It was love at first sight.

"Mama, that's what I want for Christmas! That's all I want. Really! Just that bike." Strolling over to it and straddling the seat, I ran my hands along the fringe. Felt the cool chrome of the steering. Fit my little fingers in the gold grips, perfectly made for most 6-year-olds. I had to have it.

Mama watched as I pretended to be Roy, pushing the button and listening intently to the familiar horse's whinny. Every boy from Carl to Auburn would envy my new bicycle and me.

"We'll see," was her only reply. "We'll just have to wait and see." I had heard that response many times before. It usually meant that it wouldn't really happen, that she was in hopes that I would forget all about it in time.

She pulled me from the bike and we left the store. Holding her hand and departing the Western Auto, I couldn't help but look back at the bike. Little tears ran down my cheeks. I might never see MY Trigger again.

Many weeks went by and, almost daily, I could only think about that bike. "Mama, you gonna tell Santa Claus about Trigger? You gonna let him know that I've been good? And that *THAT's* what I want for Christmas?"

"We'll see. I'm not sure he can get that big thing down the chimney. That's a mighty big gift for such a little boy."

I worried for days, thinking about that bike. I was so afraid that someone else might buy her before we could let Santa know.

Miss Rainey was my second-grade teacher. Yet another mother figure in my young life. She, like Aunt Ruby in first grade, loved children. I grew to enjoy her touch, her smile and her constant desire to teach -- and for us to learn. As we approached

Christmas break, one of her projects for us was to write letters to Santa. Mine was obvious and simple.

Dear Santa: All I want for Christmas is a Roy Rogers Trigger bike. It's at the Western Auto in Lawrenceville, Georgia. It's on the right after you go in the store. Don't put it down the chimney cause Daddy has bricked it off. Now we have just a gas stove. Be sure to be quiet, cause Daddy works hard, and he don't like to be messed with when he's asleep. Plus, I don't want you to be hollered at.

    Thank you.
    David A. Brooks, Carl, Georgia
    P.S. I been good. If you don't believe me,
    just ask Mama.

To this day, I wonder if Miss Rainey showed this letter to Mama. Even in my little head, something told me that we couldn't really afford such a gift for "Santa to bring." I also wonder now how much it cost. I'm guessing that it probably was around $20.00. Bottom line, a twenty-dollar gift for one of six children was an awful lot to spend on Christmas. I was not sure how Mama could make it happen. But I could dream, couldn't I?

Before I knew it, Christmas Eve was here. Traditionally, Jack and I were sent to bed no later than 9:00 PM. At that time, our bedroom sat in the far back corner of the house. It was the smallest room in the house. (We had yet to advance enough in the family pecking order to earn one of the larger bedrooms.) Bunk beds stood in the corner, farthest from the doorway. Though the room was small, it had two windows, one on either side of the two far walls. We shared a miniscule closet, no bigger that five feet in width, with a door no more than twenty-four inches. The closet served its purpose, storing our few clothes – jeans and shirts, together with one sport coat each.

New, white sport coats would later occupy a special place in that closet. They were like dinner jackets, handmade by our sister Sandra for Easter. What I would give to have those coats today. She was so proud to have made them for us. With our Easter jackets, we often wore to church black slacks, black bowties with white bucks. We probably resembled restaurant waiters. *This way, ladies, your table awaits.*

Sleeping on Christmas Eve was difficult at best. Jack had the top bunk, a spot I coveted. I had the lower one, where I could aggravate him to death by putting my feet up against his mattress and pushing. I especially enjoyed doing this if he had been tormenting me that particular day.

"Jack." I'd whisper. "Jack!" a little louder. "You think Mama and Daddy have gone to bed?"

"I don't think so. I can hear them movin' around." He replied. "You think they're going to be up when Santa comes? I'm afraid they might scare him away!"

"They're not going to scare him away. They got to go to bed sometime tonight. He'll come, after they turn off all the lights."

We jumped or made some sort of remark with every little sound our parents made that night. My last little task that night was praying to Jesus:

Jesus, please forgive me for hitting Jack. And for putting that frog in his shoe, and for calling him a queer, and for beating him at basketball – that one time, and for taking one of his $500 bills in Monopoly, and for putting gum in his hair while he slept, and for telling on him if he even looked at me wrong. Please, Jesus, I'm so sorry for yelling at Karen for making me cut grass that time when I didn't get the rows exactly even, and for playing with her scarves (they make great cowboy scarves), and for hitting rocks across the road with a broomstick and accidentally hitting that truck, and for telling my Mama that I didn't love her any more when she made me pull weeds in her flower bed, and for wearing my new blue jeans and rolling in cow manure, and for wearing my new penny loafers and playing king of the hill on that muddy job site up the street, and for getting mad at Aunt Ruby when she wouldn't stay home on Sunday night, so we could watch Disney, instead of going to church, and, . . .and, . . .and, . . zzzzzzzz.

I was almost always the first one up. Rolling over, I nudged Jack with my feet against the mattress underside, whispering, "Jack! Jack! Wake up! It's Christmas! Let's go see what we got?"

He'd stir and groan a little, "What time is it?"

"It's 4:30. Isn't it early enough to wake up? You think Daddy'll get mad if we wake up now and see what we got?"

Practically every day of our lives, one of Joe's children would make some sort of comment using the words *Daddy, mad* and *scared*, in the same sentence.

"He won't get mad on Christmas. Let's go open presents." We slowly moved away the covers to greet the cold room. No central heat. I can remember sometimes there being ice on the windows. The INSIDE of the windows. We both were shivering as we searched for our bathrobes in our closet. Finding them, we slid into the sleeves and tied them up, simultaneously sliding our feet into our slippers. The old wood floor would creak and yawn a little as we maneuvered through our bedroom, the little central hall, and then Aunt Ruby's room. We knew better than to go through Mom and Dad's room, for fear of waking up you-know-who.

Aunt Ruby loved Christmas. We knew if we woke her, she'd be just as childlike as us in greeting the new day, and, above all else, there was no way anyone would be upset if she was in the living room with us, opening presents.

Nudging her backside, "Aunt Ruby, Aunt Ruby. Wake up. It's Christmas! Wake up and let's open presents." She rolled over with eyes glazed. Trying to gain focus, she reached for her teeth sitting in a glass full of Provident. "What time is it?"

"It's 4:30. Time to get up."

Inside the house, it may as well been an igloo in Nome, Alaska. Aunt Ruby fumbled with her glasses and teeth, rose to the side of the bed, and took a big Brooks sigh. She laughed that high-pitched cackle we had all grown to love. We knew we had her when she did that. She rocked back and forth on the bed, then swung herself upward to a standing position. I could smell her Tussy talcum powder and Jergens body lotion that allowed me to recognize her blindfolded. Jack and I were bouncing around her bed, trying to hurry her along.

In all the years I knew her, I never saw her run or even walk fast. She mostly shuffled, and even in 1957, when she was not yet sixty, she seemed a hundred and two. She slowly worked her way around her bed, with us right behind, trying to hurry her along and not wet our pants at the same time. We no longer cared how cold it was. And brother, was it cold. Daddy had not yet gotten up to light the gas heater.

One room in our house was heated. The den was replete with Daddy's black vinyl chair that was big as an elephant, Mama's green side chair, also vinyl, with no side arms, resting next to her sewing machine. Also, Aunt Ruby's small rocker held its place next to Daddy's recliner with our dining table with four chairs and a bench pushed to one corner of the room, brought out only for mealtime. A small Philco television sat in the corner with an antenna wire crawling from its rear along the wall and out the window. It was a black and white, of course, as we didn't even know what color television was in 1957.

The old fireplace was bricked up completely below the mantel the year previous, and that large gas heater sat in front of it -- our only heat source. Daddy would normally rise each morning and light the heater long before anyone else would get up. That is, unless it was 4:30 in the morning. That old heater was also a reason to fear. Standing too close, having grandchildren walk too close, allowing too much gas to escape, setting anything on top of it, or leaning on its side were real dangers. In the summer time, it was a nice cool place to sit for me. Resting my back on its cool metal side, sitting right in front of the TV, it was like my own personal air conditioner, unless I was scolded for getting in someone's viewing space.

I could hear Aunt Ruby's fluffy slippers sliding across the tile floor as we made our way to the living room. Mama had put up the Christmas tree in the traditional place, right in front of the double windows in the front of the house, facing Highway 29.

I held tightly to Aunt Ruby's robe as Jack slipped in front of her. We were almost there. She took hold of the doorknob, turning to look at my face, then Jack's. Her greatest joy each Christmas was the faces of Joe and Nina's children. At the time, it meant nothing to me, but in my older years, I still recall with great joy myself, HER joy. She was our advocate. Our sweet Ruby.

The door was pushed open, creaking a little. Aunt Ruby swung it wide as I stepped in front, standing next to Jack. I heard her sweeping her hand across the wall in search of the light switch

Daddy had just installed. Previous to 1957, every room had simple pull-cords. Finding the switch, she snapped it upward, and light filled the space, revealing the vision.

There it was, sparkling brilliantly from the ceiling light. My Trigger. Santa had read my letter. Dreams DO come true. Not only that, but Jack had gotten a new bicycle too! His was red and chrome, looking very grown up compared to mine, but MINE was special. Very special.

We both ran over to our bikes and hopped on. Jack made engine-noises, while I knew better. Mine could only make that great sound that only Roy and I knew. "Uh-huh-huh-huh-huh-huh." The high-pitched whinny of the one and only "TRIGGER!!!!"

What a great Christmas. Jack would get a new billfold as well, some new pajamas, and a pair of blue jeans. It's not strange at all that I can't remember what else I received that Christmas. Nothing else mattered. I had my new bike, and all was well with the world.

My brother-in-law, Lawson Brady, taught me to ride a bike without training wheels. Strangely enough, I learned on Jack's bike. I guess he thought that if I could ride a larger bike, my Trigger would come a lot easier. Lawson would later become my eighth grade teacher, school Principal and my basketball coach.

Trigger had solid rubber tires. I rode that bike up and down the sidewalks of Carl and Auburn, to and from the store, to and from the Hayman house. If you saw me outside, you probably saw Trigger. That was my bicycle for many years. Even as a pre-teen, I remember having ridden out the rubber of that bike, riding only the rims. Mama would laugh at me coming down the sidewalk with sparks flying under my wheels. It was metal-on-concrete for at least a year or two. And I was really standing tall on her, having much earlier outgrown her. Trigger had long lost her tasseled fringe, her satchel and the plastic handle covers as well. Both pedals were nothing more than their center rod, and the chain came off regularly. She was missing her seat, so I dared never sit down. Ouch! There was rust here and there as well, but Trigger was still mine. It could still gallop. I could still even rear her up from time to time. Oh, how I did love that bicycle.

I suppose there's nothing to compare to a boy's first bicycle.

Heroes came and went during my childhood. I met Smiley Burnett once, during an autograph session at the Lions Club in Winder. Smiley was Gene Autry's sidekick, later one of the engineers on Petticoat Junction. Why would he come to Winder, Georgia? God only knows.

Jack and I loved "The Popeye Club" shown live out of Atlanta. Officer Don was a hero of sorts. He hosted the daily kids' show, complete with lots of Popeye cartoons, Ooey-Gooey and musical chairs. I was very thankful that the Popeye Club came to us on Channel 2. Of the three channels we received, Channel 2 came in the clearest. Channels 5 and 11 usually meant jiggling the antenna wire, playing the horizontal hold or attempting to make the "snow" go away. Often, if we wanted to watch Channel 11, my job was to sit just to the side of the TV and hold the horizontal button so that it wouldn't flip. I was happy to do it, as this made my lot in life most valuable to the family's welfare. I had a job to do, and, by George, I was going to do it!

Officer Don came to Winder once, appearing at the infamous Strand Theatre. Now demolished, the Strand and the local Dairy Queen were the centers of activity in Winder. The Oscar-Meyer Weiner-mobile was there too. Jack and I went with our Haymon cousins and sat about halfway back in the packed theatre. Somehow Jack was chosen to play Ooey-Gooey live on stage with Officer Don himself. That lucky dog! He won a sack full of prizes and snacks – Little Miss Southern Snack cakes, a wiener whistle and a Reese's peanut butter cup among them.

After the show, I was allowed about two seconds in the cockpit of the wiener mobile, after standing in line for an hour. I was even given a free whistle too. What a day! At school that Monday, it was, "I got to touch Officer Don. Would you like to touch ME?"

Eventually, cowboy and television heroes were replaced by sports heroes. I loved the Yankees, especially Mickey, Roger and Yogi. The Cardinals were a favorite as well with McIver, Bill White and Curt Flood. The Cardinals were the only team I could receive on my little transistor radio. In 1964, my two favorite teams met in the World Series. I remember wishing it would end in a tie. The Cardinals won in seven games, with Bob Gibson the winning pitcher in three of the seven. To this day, I can still recall the starting lineup of both teams. It was my Eighth grade year. Baseball was king, at least until well into October, when the Celtics took over as my fave.

I loved Bill Russell and Snatch Sanders. With Sam Jones and K.C. Jones. Wilt Chamberlain and Bill Russell matchups were unforgettable.

I remember my first University of Georgia football game: UGA vs. Florida State at Sanford Stadium. It had just rained, so getting to and from our seats included some plank walking through the areas just outside the gates. Larry Rakestraw was the Georgia quarterback. Johnny Griffith the coach. And Len Hauss our all-SEC center. Rakestraw and Mickey Babb were for the most part our entire offense. Those were the days, post-Wally Butts, that Georgia football was abysmal, but I fell in love with those silver helmets and britches. That would be, and still is, my team. It was October 20, 1962. I was about to turn eleven years old. Georgia lost 18-0. I bought a UGA pennant and waved it outside the car on the way home. My brother-in-law, Sid, who had taken me to the game, was disgusted with the results, yelling for me to, "Pull that thing in! The way they played today, I don't want anybody to know we're Georgia fans!" I didn't understand. Win or lose, I was excited to be a Georgia Bulldog.

The following year, I returned to Sanford Stadium for Georgia's annual game with Vanderbilt. The Dogs didn't disappoint, winning 20-0. I was a Bulldog for sure now.

I would listen to every game on the radio. Ed Thilenius did the play-by-play. I would hang on his every word. Later, around 1964, when new coach Vince Dooley was hired, Larry Munson became a staple. Anyone wearing the red and black instantly became a hero. Preston Ridlehuber, Kirby Moore, Lynn Hughes, George Patton, Jake Scott and Bill Stanfill. I couldn't get enough of Georgia athletics.

I cried the night the Dogs lost to Houston, the infamous duel in Knoxville, when Tennessee came back and tied the game in the last seconds. I pounded my pillow when we lost to Miami, because of a stupid cannon that went off during our only extra point try.

Thankfully though, after Dooley arrived, victories were more numerous than losses. Beating Kentucky and the Ken Norton-led Wildcats in Lexington. That miraculous victory in Athens over Alabama: Moore to Hughes to Bob Taylor. Awesome wins over SMU in the '66 Cotton Bowl. Still today, my blood runs red and black. Georgian by birth, Bulldog by the grace of God.

Football was replaced each year by basketball. I remember the day the "Coliseum" was opened. Prior to that, Georgia basketball was played in a barn of sorts, long since replaced by the Journalism Building. The Coliseum was a marvel to see, an architectural wonder. I always thought it was half-spaceship and half-bathtub. Many years later, it was ironic that during Coach Tubby Smith's tenure, it was nicknamed "The Tub."

I can recall reading about such players as Zippy Morroco, Jimmy Pitts and Jerry Waller. Later, Bob Lienhard, Dick McIntosh and Jerry Epping were stars. In 1970, as a freshman at Georgia, I was chosen as part of a PE basketball class to play against some of the varsity players and coaches. Epping and McIntosh were on the other team. We lost badly, but who cares. What a great experience.

I'm not sure why, but for some reason I was into players' numbers. I wish there was a game show that involved naming athletes' numbers from the 1950s and 60s. I'd win hands down.

Pitts #20, Stanfill #77, Scott #13. Rakestraw #10, McIntosh #11, and Moore #14,...and on and on. I not only knew the '64 World Series lineups, I can tell you their numbers too. That talent and a quarter would get you a large pack of double-bubble gum, a Reese's Cup and "Co-Cola" in 1964.

In Georgia, Coca-Cola was king. Still is. It was common to say "I'm going to get a Coke," then pick out a Nehi Grape. "Coke" was the generic term for any soda. If someone had said to me, "I'd like a soda," I would have thought they meant a bi-carbonate for stomach problems. "Soda" was a "yankee word," that meant you were highfalutin, or of the upper-crust of society. You wouldn't catch any of us saying "soda" unless it was followed by "fountain." Only then, might it refer to a "fountain Coke."

Heroes, I suppose, were part of a boy's makeup during those innocent years of the 50s and 60s. Every red-blooded American boy had several heroes, people we looked up to.

The irony of it all, though I never would have admitted it then, was the real heroes were living right there within our walls: parents, a sweet aunt and siblings whose love I still feel today, unconditionally. I didn't know that Jack would be a hero to me. That Daddy was idolized for his strength and character. That Mama would be viewed as a super-Mom. For indeed, she was. Or that Aunt Ruby would be a saint, and my sisters mothers-in-training.

Everything that I am today I owe to these eight people. The ones who held my hand, nursed my wounds and kept me out of jail. Swung from trees with me. Rode the cows. Lay with me in bed, comforting a fever or busted knee. Taught me a few carpentry skills. And, held me until I hurt. Real heroes don't really wear sports uniforms or ride horses or appear on television. Real heroes stand in our midst. I just wish I had had the wisdom then, which I do now, to have realized it.

The Brooks kindred of Carl. Heroes all.

At least to this little boy.

~ 11 ~
Sad Times

From about 1959 until her death in 1962, Sandra was the center of my parents' lives – out of necessity. It was a four-year period of dealing with cancer.

She had been born Sandra Jo Brooks on July 29, 1936, the first child of my parents, Joe and Nina.

Sandra was very outgoing and popular in high school. She was known to have a bit of fiery disposition, and would let out a pretty good yell from time to time. My memories of her are very sketchy at best. She died at the age of twenty-five, when I was only ten. By that time, Sandra and her husband Lawson had had two children: Terri and Steve, born in 1957 and '58 respectively.

I'm unsure of when Sandra was diagnosed with a cancerous brain tumor, but I remember the fear and devastation it brought to my family. Unless you or a loved one has ever experienced the ravaging nature of cancer, it's difficult to describe or understand.

My memories are for the most part filled with sadness and tears. A whole lot of tears.

I was maybe seven or eight years old when I realized something was wrong with Sandra. Mama and I were visiting her at her home in Carl, a small 3-bedroom brick ranch, built right off the highway with a semi-circular drive in front. It was simple, cute and homey. I was in the den of the home perhaps watching TV, when I realized that Sandra was having a seizure. I was young, very naïve, and seeing this for the first time was very upsetting. She lay on her bed, trembling and uttering nonsensical phrases, while Mother held a cold washcloth over her forehead. I remember Mama crying and praying aloud for Sandra to be okay. She, like every one of us, was her baby, her very first baby. Eventually, the seizure subsided, but its impact I can still feel today. It was palpable. And scary.

I remember Mama and Daddy talking about Sandra a lot. What was wrong with her? Why does she have so many headaches? What do these seizures mean? We were all puzzled, not the least of these, Lawson.

Many doctors' visits, examinations and x-rays revealed the tumor. She had cancer and she had just so long to live.

I would spend the next several years, as did my siblings, observing and contemplating the plight handed my parents, Sandra's husband and their children. Mama would be standing over the stove cooking okra, when suddenly she would just start crying. She'd wipe the tears with a washcloth hanging from her apron belt and keep on cooking. She'd be vacuuming or sweeping the house, and break out in tears. Though I was a busy little eight- or nine-year-old, interested mostly in my own little world, I couldn't help but notice what changes were going on in our mother. She was in the midst of losing one of her children forever, and was understandably coming a bit unglued. Plus, it seemed the more bad news she would receive, the busier she became around the house. And, still more tears would flow.

Throughout Sandra's illness, I never felt like Mama didn't love me and give me plenty of attention. Amazing really.

During the years leading up to her death, Sandra had several operations. There were no chemotherapy or radiation treatments in the early 60s. Each operation involved shaving her head completely, opening her skull and cutting out the tumor by hand – barbaric by today's standards. Each surgery involved weeks and weeks of physical and mental therapy. She had to learn to walk and talk all over again, following each surgery. It must have been numbing for my parents to live through.

People from all over the community helped. O. E. Herndon, proprietor of the local Carl Superette, refused to accept Lawson's payment for a month's worth of groceries. Mary Healan helped by babysitting Terri and Steve on countless occasions. Church folk provided many meals for the family. The ladies circle of Carl Baptist even paid for a young African-American lady to come once or twice a week to help with laundry, babysitting and general housework. Gussie was a sweet soul who loved Sandra so much and did quite a bit to make Jack's and my life, and especially Mama's life, a bit easier. She also would go to Sandra and Lawson's house to help them as well. God bless her. I think often of her sacrifices, being away from her own family, to assist us.

Sandra's last days were spent at Our Lady of Perpetual Help Convalescent Home in south Atlanta, one of the first "hospices" to be developed in Georgia. The Roman Catholic sisters there became like family to Mom and Dad. And to us as well. Though never fully understanding the Catholic faith, Mama learned to like and respect what they stood for, in their care and love for the dying. Sister Amelda was a special friend of Mama's and of Sandra's. Long after Sandra's death, she and Mama would correspond on a regular basis. I later discovered that the good Sister had retired and returned to her home in Minnesota. She passed away in the early 1990s.

Sandra occupies a small part of my memories. Her lengthy illness meant lots of long hours and days witnessing my parents in emotional turmoil. I never fully understood what was going on. That someone so young could actually die. Leave us forever. Many weekends were spent with us going to whatever hospital or home where Sandra was. Jack and I witnessed lots of sadness in those days.

Sandra died on April 25, 1962. Jack and I slept in the back bedroom recently left unoccupied by our sisters Dorian and Karen. Mama came in early that morning, shook us awake, and quietly said, "Get up boys. Quietly put your clothes on and get ready for the day. Sandra died last night." She turned, wiped a tear away and walked out of the room.

Just as quickly as that, she was gone. Jack cried aloud, rolling in the bed. He defiantly pounded the pillow. I just lay there. Not speaking. Not crying. Just wondering about the days ahead, and what was to occur. The funeral. Lots of food. People visiting.

And of course, more tears. It was a cold, spring morning. Jack and I were both under several blankets. I assembled my clothes for the day, maneuvering my way to the nicely heated den to put them on.

I remember standing near the television in the back of the room, when Ms. Parder came rushing through the room from the front door, hugging Aunt Ruby and Mama. Thankfully, she didn't notice me struggling with my jeans, modestly pulling them up to my waist and adjusting the fly. She had stopped on her way to school to offer her condolences -- a word I would become very familiar with over the next few days.

There were times over the next few days when Mama and Daddy would cry hysterically, especially Mama. I know now that they had lost one of their babies. In fact the one with whom they had set up housekeeping. They had learned to be parents together with Sandra as their first doll. My stomach would turn several flips each time I saw them so upset.

I remember thinking about how sad this all was. About the great food we would eat. About how I got to miss several days of school. About all the cousins, aunts and uncles that soon appeared at our doorstep. It was all so very strange to me. A complete cornucopia of emotions.

My parents would never be the same after that cold day in April. They both ceased to be active in their Church. They questioned things, especially God. Understandably so. How could this happen? Why, God? How could you leave a three- and two-year-old motherless? And a husband a widower? Why? How? Answer us! Explain this pain! Give us some reason! Please!

None of my siblings would ever be the same either. Including Sandra's husband Lawson. And most assuredly, neither would I.

It is said that it's "your faith that gets you through times like this." Sometimes, I'm not so sure about that.

But then again, something got us through it…so it must be true after all.

It must be faith.

~ 12 ~
Connie Frances and Me

As a kid, I loved having older married sisters. It gave me a place to visit. A place to get away from the hum-drum life of Carl. Life that really didn't seem that boring, until I got away for a few days.

Marilyn, sister number two, lived with her husband in an upstairs apartment near Agnes Scott College in Decatur, Georgia. The year was 1959. The most memorable characteristic about her apartment was the outside catwalk to and from its front entrance. What a cool thing to have!

She was gorgeous, with red, wavy hair. I thought all my sisters hung the moon. Marilyn was no exception. I grew to respect and love women, by watching all the women in my life, for there were many, but especially her. She seemed very much in control of things. Headstrong. Working as a Registered Nurse via Georgia Baptist School of Nursing, housework and raising children were all part of her juggling act. She was the closest sister to Sandra, and probably most affected by her death. She not only lost a sibling, but her best friend as well.

I loved visiting Marilyn and her husband, Sid. It provided adventure to such exotic places as Tuscumbia, Alabama and Festus, Missouri where they lived. Going to Festus was like traveling to the other side of the world, at least in my little mind.

Marilyn invited Jack and me for a weekend visit when she and Sid lived in the apartment in Decatur. I was so excited, because as part of the stay, we were going to a movie. Now, keep in mind that going to a movie was a really big deal. Up until that date, I had seen only two movies, both at Winder's Strand Theatre: "Gone With The Wind" and "Ben Hur." On this particular day, not only were we going to a movie, but also it was to include a trolley ride into downtown Atlanta and a show at the famed Fox Theatre. I couldn't wait. It didn't matter what movie was playing. The prospects of experiencing new things were all that mattered.

I was eight years old at the time. Growing up with lots of siblings and lots of adults in the house, we experienced our first indoor bathroom when I was five. That was the place where I quickly learned I could be most private. It was quiet. When the window was open, there was a nice breeze. And that nice potty seat was incredibly cool and comfortable – important features in a house with no air conditioning. It beat the heck out of the old two-holer we had some 50 yards behind the house. Still to this day, I never understood why we had a two-holer. Who in their right mind wants to sit next to someone else and do that!!!???

I detested our school bathrooms. In eight years of schooling at Auburn Elementary and four years at Winder-Barrow High School, I never once relieved myself in those bathrooms – except to do good old number one. So you can imagine what the first thing I did each day upon my return home. The bathrooms at church were awful too. While in there, you could hear everything that went on in the hallway and in the two adjoining Sunday School rooms too. Besides, you could never be certain that the door really locked, and the door itself had at least a 3-inch crack between its bottom and the floor. No way was I ever going to leave a little piece of me in that place! I even disliked going to the bathroom at my sisters' places. It just didn't feel right. Our little 4 x 8 bathroom in Carl was *the* place for me. Besides, who wants to be made fun of for stinking up somebody else's place?

I remember wearing my favorite jeans that day. Dorian and Karen met us at the theatre. What a treat. We wore our new flannel shirts too, mine blue and his red-plaid. We liked to roll our jeans legs up 3 or 4 inches as well. White socks and penny loafers rounded out the ensemble. Were we ever the coolest! No one could tell that we were country bumpkins from Carl…Yeah, right.

We rode the trolley from Decatur to Atlanta. It rolled down Ponce de Leon Avenue, letting us off right in front of the Fox. I was really something, as I stepped out of the trolley, peering up and down busy Peachtree Street. People were everywhere. To and fro. Rushing to get somewhere obviously important. I would need to be on my best behavior, for I was sure everyone was looking at me. But no red carpet? Don't these people know who I am. I travelled over fifty miles to be here!

Straining my neck to look up at the Fox's marquee, I could read very plainly what we were about to see: "Where The Boys Are," starring Connie Frances.

"Where The Boys Are???" Come on! How about Roy Rogers or Gene Autry or The Lone Ranger? At the tender age of eight, I was being introduced to what "chick flick" meant. Oh well. Who really cared any way. I'm away from home, all dressed up, ready to see a movie on the big screen. Bring on the Fireball jawbreakers, candy bars and popcorn.

There is practically nothing as good as buttered popcorn at the theatre. And what about chocolate raisinettes? Wow, could those two things set my mouth to watering. And Coke too! Lots and lots of "Co-Cola."

Coca-Cola was a very special treat for all us Brooks kids. I recall when they first came out with the large "family size" bottles of Coke. Our Sunday night ritual in the summer was usually off to Sunday night church, home by 8:30 after a quick stop at O.E. Herndon's Carl Superette. Daddy would buy a large bottle of Coke for all of us to share.

We'd gather on the front porch, with traffic whizzing by. The two front-porch lights drew every bug in Carl, and they came in droves, diving headlong into the screens protecting us from their awful stings. House plants sat along the concrete shelf that lined the two outer walls. Two swings sat side by side, and an assortment of rockers and benches were scattered about, all facing out to that gorgeous view of Highway 29.

Jack and I would roll out the old round card table from behind one of the swings and maneuver it between the rockers. Daddy would place the large bottle of Coke in the middle of the table. Mother would appear carrying an enormous round tray with several glasses filled with ice. Typically, the glasses were ones she had earned with Blue Horse Trading Stamps or by purchasing gas at the local Gulf Oil store. Daddy would pop the top on the big bottle and place it back down, with the smoke rising from its cold interior. I sat on the large rocker and leaned forward, head resting on my hands, elbows outstretched, staring at the prize. That bottle was like a Mayan god, and we were its worshipers.

I couldn't wait to set my lips to the glass's edge and sip away. He would pour each of us a glass. Taking mine, I would retreat to one of our swings, hold the glass with both hands, slowly sipping at the sweet soda, savoring each droplet. I would always pride myself at being the last to finish my Coke. I could nurse an eight-ounce glass of Coke for a good two hours before it would be all gone. Ah, one of life's simple, little pleasures.

Fountain Cokes at the theatre were sweeter still. We entered the movie house and quickly purchased our usual fare: large popcorn and medium Coke. Taking our seats, I began to munch away, taking a sip from my Coke on occasions. The movie began. To this day, I have no idea what it was about. But I'll never forget the food. My popcorn was followed quickly by a medium box of chocolate-covered raisins, then who can live without a box of Milk-Duds. And oh, those hot dogs smelled so good; I just had to try one of those covered in onions. Another Coke or two followed by some cotton candy, a Milky Way and a bag of peanuts and I had just about done The Fox Theatre. By now, I think you're getting the picture as to why I enjoyed being away from home.

The movie ended. With credits rolling, the lights came up slowly and we rose to leave. I looked down on the floor around my seat. It looked like a small nuclear device had gone off. But, oh what a day. Every imaginable treat known to man had entered my system that afternoon, in the space of about two hours.

We strolled up the aisle towards the exit, when it hit me. "Boi-oi-oi-oi-oing!!!" My stomach began to make every sound known to medical science. I could literally feel the Coke and various junk foods swirling around inside. My entire insides were doing triple half gainers followed by a double somersault. I had to go to the bathroom. Boy, did I have to go! All I could think about was, "Get me to that bathroom!"

Marilyn pointed Jack and me toward the men's room. Men's room? I don't need a men's room! I need a little boy's room. Something akin to my little 4 x 8 space in Carl! I don't need no stinkin' men's room!

We entered, and I immediately realized we were in a man's world...not to be confused with a boys world. This was definitely NOT my little bathroom back in Carl. There were urinals on the side, much taller that I could ever reach with any body part I had, and several stalls across the way. Jack stepped up to the urinal and did his thing, and I ducked inside a stall. Fumbling with the lock, I secured my private space, unzipped and quickly sat down to do my business. But nothing happened. I mean literally, nothing!

Several minutes went by. I became more and more anxious. Here I was in a public place, about to smell up the entire northern suburbs of Atlanta, with my stomach imitating a premature volcanic eruption, and nothing happened! What the heck was going on? How could this be?

I began to sweat. My feet went numb. Jack was knocking on the stall. "David! Hurry up. We gotta go!" And for the first time to my knowledge, I became intimately aware of something I would later learn to be "anal retentive." I couldn't go. My lower abdomen was yelling out for help, but my brain was having none of it. What a strange and very new sensation! A tear or two rolled down my cheek, and I began to pray for God to either provide me relief, or lead me magically home.

"David! Come on! What are you doing in there?" Jack yelled again. Now surely everyone in the bathroom knew of my personal travails. I could only imagine some fool old man at the urinals, turning to his buddy and laughing, "Hey, Bill, some punk's in the john and can't go! He must be a cracker from Carl! Probably never been in a real bathroom before!"

It was no use. I stood up, zipped up and prepared to leave the bathroom, with my stomach yelling out to me, "You fool! Where are you going? You gotta take care of this! Get back in that stall!"

Jack took my hand and we left the men's room. No one, except God and I knew what was going on with me. I was totally mortified, and my stomach continued to remind me that there would be no relief in sight, at least not until our long trolley ride back to Decatur. I prayed to myself, "God, please let me make it to Marilyn's apartment. Please, just this once, let me make it. I promise I'll never lie, cheat or steal ever again – not that I had ever done any of those things anyway, not one of Joe Brooks's kids.

I sat next to Jack in the trolley. He had the window seat with me on the aisle. The old trolley rocked and rolled up and down Ponce, taking its bloody time back to Decatur. I felt every little bump. With every stop to allow passengers to enter and exit, I wanted to run up to the driver and yell, "For God's sake would you hurry up!" and then turn to the other passengers and announce, "There will be no more stops until we get to Agnes Scott College!"

I became very much aware of every curve on Ponce de Leon that day. And there were many. We finally made it to our stop and exited the bus. Every little step down the sidewalk was oh so painful. I can recall almost passing out from the pain. I thought about the bathroom back at the Fox. I thought about the slow ride home. Taking itty-bitty, baby steps, I tried to think about anything that might take my mind off my pressing bowel needs.

We were close now.

"Why in the world couldn't the bus have let us off closer to home? For that matter, why couldn't the bus have a bathroom on board? Why didn't I go, back at the Fox? Why did I have to devour so much junk at the movies? Why? Why? Why?"

And then it happened. Right there in Decatur, Georgia, on the campus of Agnes Scott College.

Eight years old! Oh my God, just take a gun and shoot me now. Marilyn sensed my catastrophic state. Who wouldn't sense my state? I just sat down, began to cry, and try my best to make sense of it all. Please hand me a shovel so I can start digging my grave. Please just leave me here; I'll just crawl back into the woods and make a whole new life for myself.

I owe Marilyn, big time. She was the cleanup crew.

Also to this day, I can never think of Connie Frances, hear one of her songs, be reminded of that girls college in Decatur, or ride a trolley, without breaking out in a cold sweat.

Now, you might be thinking, in the words of Lewis Grizzard, "Damn, brother, I don't think I'da told that." The fact is that writing it down allows me a certain sense of relief. Relief precisely like I needed that day in 1959.

So, please don't mention that God-awful movie to me, ever. Instead of "Where The Boys Are," they should have named it, "Where the Boy Wasn't."

In the Fox Theatre bathroom where he belonged.

~ 13 ~
Train Meets Car

Unfortunately, the railroad *did* mean death to some.

It was the summer of 1966. I was working my first real paying job at the local pants manufacturing company in the "twin cities" (Carl/Auburn). R&R Manufacturing was located just across the highway and railroad tracks, so walking to and from work for lunch was extremely convenient.

I finished my workday at 5:00, walked home and sat at the kitchen table, talking about my day of being a "bundle boy" or "fly presser." I was especially happy this day, as I had "made production." That meant that I had pressed over 1,200 pairs of pants that day, and anything over that meant a few pennies above the going minimum wage of $1.60 per hour. R&R was a men's pants manufacturer. Making a weekly salary was pretty dog gone special.

Dad soon pulled in, parked his Chevy truck, quickly washed up and was sitting at the table as well. Aunt Ruby always sat on one end. Dad on the other. Mom and I faced one another at the side-table. Looking back, it's funny how people claim their space when it comes to eating or watching TV, or whatever.

Salmon patties were the fare of the day. Mama would on occasion fry them on the stovetop and serve them with home made biscuits, mashed potatoes and fresh green beans. There might be two or three other vegetables from leftovers of previous suppers.

A large glass of sweet tea would round off the one-course extravaganza. Daddy had stirred his tea and we were digging in.

I remember it being extremely hot. So what else was new? Since we ate in the little kitchen where Mama had just cooked, the heat was still very present in the room. The window was open, and the back door leading to the screened porch was propped open. The breeze was barely noticeable. Most every day during supper, a fly would come in from the back porch and dodge-and-weave Mama's dishrag attempt at eliminating the nuisance. Just another day in paradise.

I had just forked off a nice piece of salmon when we each realized a train was approaching from the east, headed toward Lawrenceville and eventually Atlanta. Instead of its usual high-pitched "toot-toot!" there was this long drawn-out blaring of its horn. If a car, it would be akin to someone "sitting" on the horn.

Then, WHAM!

The table and house shook. I looked up at Daddy and Mama. "Oh my God!" Mama shouted.

The noise of train-meets-car was unlike anything I had ever heard. A horrible crash followed by a rolling rumble somewhat like thunder. I got up quickly, racing through the den and out the front door. Peering across the road, I could see a car turned upside down in the ditch between the highway and railroad. Its rear wheels were still spinning. A cloudy combination of grass, dust and smoke had gathered around the area.

A grief-stricken panic came on me. Taking a quick glance up and down the road, I streaked across the heat-laden pavement, each stride bringing me closer and closer to a sight that still lingers in my head.

There had been three people in the car. They had obviously just been to the grocery store. A loaf of white bread was scattered throughout. There was a small package of bologna, a jar of mayonnaise, some celery, paper napkins and all other shapes and varieties of items found in most grocery aisles.

A large woman lay on her back. Her white sundress lay limp on her frame. Her head seemed to be facing in the opposite direction of her body. Her arms and legs looked unnatural as well. Both her shoes were missing. Her hair had remnants of grass and briars scattered within. I stood over her and kneeled down to provide assistance, then thought better of it. Standing quickly, I looked back across the road to see Mom and Dad standing just outside the front door.

"Bring some blankets!" I called out. It was the only thing I could think of to do. Mom turned and raced back into the house.

"Call an ambulance! Quick!" I directed Dad. It was the first time in my life I had ever told my Dad what to do. He responded directly, as a rush of responsibility and "being in charge" came over me.

Realizing she most certainly was killed instantly, I turned away from this poor woman and noticed a man who seemed much younger lying on his side. His shirttail was out, and one or two buttons from his shirt had appeared to be ripped from their buttonholes. He too, was covered in dirt and grass. A faint and eerie moan came from his upper body. I knelt down and took one hand, attempting to provide what little comfort I knew how. "Hang in there buddy. You're going to be alright. Just keep breathing. Hang in there." I was holding his palm with one hand and gently patting and rubbing with the other – something my Mother had done for me countless times before. Allowing my eyes to move down to his legs, I saw for the first time something I'd never seen before. His left leg had been sheered off cleanly at his mid-calf. Blood was gushing out onto the sand and gravel of the railway bed where he lay. His moaning continued. He never spoke. Just moaned. It was the unforgettable sound of impending death.

I took off my shirt, tying it around the open wound of his leg in a futile attempt to stop the bleeding. I knew this couldn't hurt and just might keep him from bleeding to death. Looking down again at him, I continued to try and provide some degree of comfort. Looking around, I saw his missing foot, still with its shoe tied securely to a white sock. My face went flush. My mind, numb. I shook my head to bring myself back to what had just occurred. Glancing east, I noticed yet another body tangled in the briars and weeds that made up the trench between the railroad and highway. A car stopped. I recognized John Rainey, the youngest son of my Second Grade teacher and family friend from Carl. He stepped up on the rise near our mailbox and called out, "Are they OK?"

"No! Not at all! I think those two are gone, and this one's hanging on."

Mother appeared beside me. "Oh my God!" she exclaimed, putting her hand to her mouth. I could see a faint tear well up in her eyes. An upsetting sight would be very much an understatement.

Dad soon reappeared at the scene, seeing the third body as well, some twenty yards closer to the initial contact point. It was an older man. He was missing one arm, and his head was opened. His brain was exposed, glistening with body fluid and blood. He too was missing his shoes, and his pants had somehow been pulled down around his mid-thigh.

The impact had come with such force that the car had rolled over multiple times, stopping one-hundred yards or so west of the railroad crossing. Along its tumbling journey, the car had ejected its occupants, possibly being thrown out and struck again by the train, or rolled upon by the car.

Imagine an explosion involving a car and its three occupants. That's what the scene reminded me of. A bomb had gone off in the form of a multi-ton locomotive moving at a high rate of speed.

An ambulance soon pulled up to the scene. By the time of its arrival, fifty or sixty people were gathered around the sight. Several people had pulled into our front drive, or simply onto the side of the road. The train itself had stopped much further west. I had recognized the release of its brakes. The engineer had exited the locomotive and was making his way in our direction. A look of despair and helplessness seemed to be in his walk. The train sat motionless, creaked and moaned a little, as if to be asking forgiveness in its powerful stillness.

A short time later, three ambulances came and left with the three bodies, one still living, only to die the next morning. One of the paramedics walked the wreckage, bagging body parts. It amazed me how he collected legs and arms with so little emotion – almost like he was picking up firewood. A tow truck pulled the car upright, and off it went. The curious crowd departed, having nothing more at which to stare. Mom, Dad and I gathered again at the kitchen table to finish eating. But I couldn't eat. None of us could. Mama and Aunt Ruby gathered together the unfinished plates and began to put away the untouched food for another meal. Another time.

The reality of what we had just experienced began to sink in. I stared at my unfinished dinner. Everything else about life seemed so unimportant. A big dose of reality and perspective overcame me. Who cares about summer jobs, or salaries, or making production. For that matter, for food to eat and flies to swat.

"Mom, Dad, I'd like for us to pledge right now, that whether there's a gate or not, we *ALWAYS* stop at railroad crossings. I would never want anyone that I care about to die like that."

My eyes swelled a little. A tiny droplet ran down my cheek, spilling onto my plate. I swallowed hard. Placed my napkin on the table and strolled out to the dog pen.

We *all* took the pledge that day. And, we all said a little prayer for that unfortunate family of three.

~ 14 ~
Characters of Carl

Delvin and Wanda Thompson were neighbors. Their tumultuous, and sometimes sad relationship provided much entertainment for us Brookses. And much guilt today.

They would scream at each other at the top of their lungs, in the middle of some serious domestic dispute. The Thompson family was a large family, having six children. Just like us. They struggled to make ends meet. Just like us. And sometimes the children looked like orphans. Just like us. Their arguments would often stretch out into their front yard, where they most assuredly would see the nosy stares of the Brooks children.

Delvin sold auto parts. He owned one car and spent lots of time gardening. Just like us. Wanda worked as a part-time seamstress for the tiny community. Just like mama.

I loved the hand-painted signs in front of Mr. Delvin's garage. "Ingines Re-Werked" read one of the signs. And "Privit Propurty, Keep Of." It was funny to our little brains, but thinking on it now, they were doing the best they knew how. What right was it for us to judge?

Delvin was typical of many inhabitants in rural Georgia. Poorly educated, some not at all. Others knew only what they had been told or taught by their parents. However, in my later years, he was very helpful in teaching me how engines ran and how to change the oil in my beloved 1964 Chevelle, kindly sold to me by my youngest sister Karen, for the tidy sum of $300. Driving the country roads of Barrow County, with the opportunity to get away, became critical to my happiness meter at an early age. It was like a bad habit, albeit a harmless one.

Wanda herself had a bad habit as well.

During the 1950s, there seemed to be lots and lots of troop movement. Standing out on the sidewalk, one could see dozens of passenger train cars over a week's time transporting troops. Post World War II, the Cold War and later Cuba were all potential boiling points, regarding our safety and welfare. I can only assume this was why troops were so visible. It was not unusual to see military convoys on the highway once or twice a month.

Wanda loved to step out in her front yard and wave at the troops and sometimes the engineer. This really wasn't that unusual. I waved a lot to them, too. Sometimes I'd even salute, like a good little soldier in hopes that one would return the courtesy.

It wasn't so much why Wanda waved, but HOW she waved.

She'd stand near the tracks just short of the railway bed, lift up her skirt and apron, ever so slightly, and wave like mad. I would always know she was out doing her thing, because I could see the troops all standing up to get a good look. They probably couldn't believe their eyes. Or, maybe they could.

On a few occasions too, when the train was stopped for switching, she'd come running out alongside the train and collect notes the troops would toss out the train cars' open windows. I often pondered what in the world did they have to say to her that was so all-fired important?

Life must have been pretty miserable for Wanda. In many ways, she was a typical "lady of the house" who was overwhelmed by childcare responsibilities and a husband who probably did not share in that burden. Uneducated. Poor. She never harmed anyone to my knowledge. Nor did Delvin.

I felt sorry for them. I wondered openly if they were really loved. Though I questioned a few times whether or not *I* was loved too. For at the end of the day, I knew I was. For sure.

Delvin and Wanda stayed together through the many years, though life was hard for them. I recognized their hardships and their problems. It made me realize that we weren't so poor after all. We were, in fact, a lot like them. We were loved unconditionally, and that we were fortunate in our plight. I'm sure the Thompson children were loved just as much in theirs.

For it wasn't a plight at all. Just families getting by. In survival mode.

"It's tough to thrive, when you're in survival mode." Someone once said.

We only knew her as Dora. She and her family lived nearby. She was a palm reader, with a huge vertical sign planted in front of her house near Highway 29. We rarely saw her. She was in many ways a mystery. There were children in and around the house, but I never saw a man. I often wondered just how much business she could possibly do? Who were her customers? What is palm reading all about?

Mother would joke to friends whenever someone would question the weather, or raise a curiosity about any community or world events. She'd remark, "I don't know; maybe go ask Dora."

Jack and I were biking toward Auburn one Saturday morning. That is he was on the seat while I sat sidesaddle on the bar. Normally, Dora's big sign warranted no attention from us. It was just part of the "scenery."

Suddenly Jack slowed to a stop, peering upward, "Would'ya look at that!"

Dora's sign was a large, white hand, palm out, hand-painted on a red background. There were small yellow stars and a larger waxing crescent moon. The hours of operation were plainly printed near the bottom. We stared at the disfigured hand.

Someone had taken red paint and painted over one-half of three fingers, leaving only the middle finger intact. We laughed out loud. "Who do you think did it?" I asked.

"I don't' know," Jack replied, "But I can give you a pretty good guess."

We never discovered the culprits. Whomever it was never uttered a word, at least that got back to us. News spread quickly that the sign had been tampered with. The local police soon appeared, wandering around the area of the sign. I suppose they were searching for clues, footprints, tire prints, whatever they could find.

Later that day, I saw Dora sitting atop a large stepladder. She was in her early sixties. Long braided hair. An ankle-length, cotton skirt and mismatched sweater and blouse. Black ankle socks and bedroom shoes finished off the ensemble. She appeared to be somewhat soiled and unkempt. Probably a lot like Jack and I looked. In the kingdom of Carl, she likely was several steps below "middle class." Probably a lot like the Brookses.

She was visibly upset, but was trying her best to right the wrong inflicted on her that day. She slowly and carefully retraced the still visible lines outlining each finger, bringing it back to its original state.

It made me sad that here was this poor woman simply trying to make a living, only to tolerate someone's cruel deed. It made me sad to see her working so hard. It made me sad that we had laughed at the sign earlier.

Eventually, she finished.

Dora's Palm Reading was back in business.

We loved our neighbor, Ms. Hardegree. She was a widow who lived just to the other side of Aunt Ruby. She probably was in her late seventies when we were children. She lived in a large, old wooden structure with a wide front porch. Her yard was dirt. We often saw her sweeping her yard with an old stick broom, clearing it of leaves and debris.

She had china berry trees all around her property. We loved to take the hard berries, insert them into a sling shot and propel them toward some bird or squirrel. Toward one another, too. They could leave a mighty whelp on your backside. One of the tree's overhanging limbs stood some twenty to twenty-five feet off the ground and draped far over the highway. Climbing out onto the limb could place you directly above passing cars and trucks. We'd take a handful of berries, climb out and wait for a passing semi-truck. Just as its long trailer was directly below, we'd drop the berries down onto its roof. What a deafening, echoing sound it would make. Thankful I am that we didn't cause any harm to vehicles or drivers. Or to us.

A few steps from her back door sat a covered, open-sided well. We called it her well house. She never had indoor plumbing until the late 1950s. A wonderful treat in the summer was to go to Ms. Hardegree's house, knock on her back door, and ask her for some "well water." She would slowly slide-step her way down her back stoop, make her way to the well and begin to turn the crank/handle of the rope post, to lower the wooden bucket downward. We could hear it contacting the water. She'd wait a second of two allowing the water to fill the bucket, and then crank the bucket back up. Upon its appearance above the well wall, she'd take a long-handled, aluminum dipper and dip out some of the cold, cold elixir. Ah, well water. Nothing like it on a hot, summer day.

Such a simple pleasure, yet we loved it so.

Some two miles from our home lived Mr. and Mrs. Dwight Logan. Mr. Logan was seen regularly walking up and down the sidewalks of Carl, but Mrs. Logan was only seen on Sundays. I'll explain later.

Mr. Logan worked at the pants manufacturing plant across from our house. He would walk each day to and from work. Always wearing denim overalls and a plaid shirt. Even the few times he appeared at church, he'd still be wearing overalls, except with a white shirt and necktie tucked neatly under the bib.

He was a kind man, but a little quirky in his mannerisms.

Their house stood along the Midway Church Road. It was a tiny structure. Unpainted, weathered wood and a mixture of tin and shingles as its roof. Like Mrs. Hardegree, their yard was also dirt, with no speck of grass or weeds to be seen. A nicely shaped stick broom leaned against the side of the house. Chickens were everywhere.

The house stood on four columns of stacked rock with the front porch barely attached to the main part of the house. Observing the structure reminded me of the real meaning of a "lean-to."

Every year, around September, Mr. Logan would buy a new Chevrolet. Usually a smaller model, such as a Chevy Nova, Belair or Chevelle. He always dealt with Ouzts Chevrolet in Winder, and at trade-in time each year, it's doubtful his car had 1,000 miles.

Next to his house was a matching garage. It too would barely pass inspection. The car stayed in that garage practically all the time. He'd pull it into the tiny building, and then walk back out to swing two hinged doors that met in the middle. A large lock would then be clamped onto the garage door handles. Nothing was going to touch, see or steal his precious Chevy.

Six days a week, Mr. Logan would leave the car in its cozy garage, walking everywhere he needed to go. Sunday was their special day. Every Sunday without fail, he and Mrs. Logan would march out to the garage. He'd back it out into the yard. She'd enter the passenger side, and they would go on their "Sunday drive."

Their ritual route would usually take them to Auburn, the neighboring town of Bethlehem, and the unincorporated areas of Whistleville, County Line and Harbins. I might see them pass our house three times on any given Sunday. He'd always toot his horn and wave. It was a bit like he wanted everyone to see him in his shiny new car.

On one particular Sunday, Jack and I were playing pitch between our house and aunt Ruby's. We were standing some 20 yards apart, throwing the baseball back-and-forth as we had done a hundred times before. Jack stood near mother's flower garden and I was positioned near the highway, with my back to the road. We were both decent throwers and could usually hit our mark pretty well. Except for this one particular time. Jack could throw a baseball much faster than I. So when one of his throws would hit the ground before its arrival, I might very well duck to one side. Otherwise, the little white sphere might find its way between my legs or into my two front teeth.

So when one of his throws found the dirt in front of me, I immediately ducked, and the ball went flying on to Highway 29.

"Pow!" went the ball, directly against the side of a vehicle passing by. The car slowed but never stopped. I wondered aloud if we might be in trouble, but since the car continued on, we both hoped that no damage was done.

About one week went by, and we were sitting at the family dinner table. Peas and cornbread as I recall. Daddy was stirring his 32-ounce glass of iced tea, complete with 4 tablespoons of sugar and an entire lemon. He had that look he got when he was about to make a pronouncement.

"So boys, guess who I ran into today?"

We both looked up from our plates and froze. We knew very well that Voice tone. We were very familiar with the way in which he posed the question. We were in trouble. What on earth did we do this time?

"Mr. Dwight told me that last Sunday, as he was driving by our house, something came flying out of our yard and put a nice dent in the side of his new Chevy."

My heart sank. Jack's face turned red. Mine too probably. Of all the cars we could've hit that day, why did it have to be Mr. Logan's?

There were many times when Daddy would be angered by our dumb actions, but for some reason, this time he wasn't.

Daddy continued, "He said the ball did some $75 worth of damage. I tried my best to pay him for his trouble, but he refused to take it. Said it was an accident. And, accidents happen."

To this day, I'm still not 100% certain that Daddy was telling the whole story. There's part of me that says he paid Mr. Logan the money that day. And part of me says he's telling the whole truth.

Anyway, The entire episode ended with a light scolding and an insistence that we never throw the ball near the highway again.

We dug into our black-eyed peas, and thanked our lucky stars.

Our Little town of Carl was full of odd characters. (Uh, like the Brookses?) Most were loving, caring, kind and generous souls. God fearing folk who were just trying to make it and get along. God knows, some of these fine people thought *we* were quite odd too.

Every level of society could be found in Carl. It's what made our town what it was. And many of those characters helped shape the Barrow's children into what they would become. Likewise, what we Brookses would become.

And thankfully, that's not all bad.

~ 15 ~
A Whole Lotta Bull

A large pecan tree stood between our house and Aunt Ruby's. Slightly off to one side and near the septic-tank-fed fig bush, this tree was a point of pride.

"Our pecan tree is the biggest tree in Barrow County." I'd say to my classmates. There always followed argument from one or two friends whose trees were equally important to them, and certainly just as big.

Daddy loved trees. He planted pecan trees throughout our back yard, along with a wide assortment of fruit trees. Every time he'd plant another tree, all I could think about was just another object to maneuver the lawn mower around. But after the tree grew for a few years and on days when we'd seek out a mid-day snack, we didn't go in the house in search of an Oreo or Little Debbie. We sauntered over to a fruit tree for a readymade treat. Apples, pears, plums, pecans, and even blackberries were plentiful. Later on in life, Daddy was proud of the grape vines he planted in the pasture. I sometimes long for those days again.

The trunk of the big pecan tree was about five to six feet in diameter. Its bark was thick with crevices large enough to vanish a fingernail. Its lowest limbs were fifteen to twenty feet from the ground, making it not the most accessible object for climbing. Those limbs stretched out in every direction, and with their weight would hang down almost reaching the ground.

One particular limb, about two feet in diameter at its base, reached far beyond the tree's trunk and was covered with leaves and pecans. It made the perfect limb for attaching a rope for a swing. And swing we did. For a while, we had the typical tire swing, but much later, it simply became a swing with a perfect step-in loop. We would take the loop-end of the rope, put it in our mouths, carefully climb up the overhanging limb to which it was attached, place one foot in the loop and away we'd go. To our little minds, no State Fair ride could have equaled the fun-factor that swing gave us. We'd swing so high; we'd almost touch the roof on the back of the house.

A rope swing generally would last us a summer. By Thanksgiving, it would have broken. Heaven forbid I would be the one on it when it did.

That limb served another purpose as well. That was to hoist a pulley chain, for slaughtering pigs, cows or anything else we might have chosen to raise and harvest.

From the time I remember, we had animals: dogs, of course, but also milk cows, bulls, chickens and pigs. At about age five, we ceased to have milk cows, chickens and pigs. Just bulls.

Purchasing a baby bull was an all-day experience. Prior to 1964, Daddy never owned a truck. We were a one-car family. On days when Daddy was working with his nephew and good friend Otis Haymon at a construction site, they would ride together, leaving the car with Mama and us the ability to "go places."

Without a truck, we would use the family sedan to drive to our Uncle Emmitt's in Walton County to purchase a bull – for the huge sum of $18. Uncle Emmitt was a dairy farmer. When one of his prize milk cows gave birth to a bull, he would sell it straightaway. He kept only one or two adult males on his farm. It was much later that I finally figured out why. "He was a dairy farmer for goodness sake! Why does he need bulls?" my little mind thought.

Uncle Emmitt Brooks and his wife, my Aunt Mary Ellen, lived with their oldest child, Geneva Garmon and her daughter, Charlotte. Though Geneva was my first cousin, Charlotte was my contemporary. As explained in chapter 9, she and I were like two peas in a pod. She was my shadow. And I hers.

The Emmitt Brookses lived in a small four-room house with adjoining back and front porches. There was an old clapboard barn resting to one side of the property, and some fifty yards to the rear was the dairy barn. Uncle Emmitt was a serious dairy farmer to my way of thinking. Never had I seen so many head of cattle in one pasture.

Emmitt would typically call his younger brother, Joe, to tell him when he had a bull to sell. Most of the time, Dad would take him up on his offer, and our day-trip to Walton County would be planned. We drove along unmarked paved roads to his farm, past fields of un-baled hay, kudzu and tall poplars. The road wound and turned over small creeks and bridges. Though only a twenty-minute drive, it was an adventure.

Our mode of transportation was a 1960 Chevrolet Impala. This would be the car I would later learn to drive. For this day, it was our calf-hauler.

Jack and I were always eager to see our latest acquisition. For the next year or so, it would be our pet. Most times, the calf would be a Jersey or "commercial" breed. Occasionally it would be a white-faced Hereford.

A calf's eyes always transfixed me. Dark, mirror-like lenses were topped by long curving eyelashes. Their hide had an attractive, newborn smell, very soft to the touch. It was like winning a stuffed animal at the Winder Fair, only this one was living and breathing…and doing something else.

As soon as the calf was taken from the barn, it began to bleat. Its mother would be visibly upset as well. Daddy would take the calf's tail in one hand and its ear in another, guiding it toward the car. It would struggle and cry aloud, while the mother had a very anxious, worried look while bending her head and neck out the barn door's upper half. My feelings about taking an animal away from its mother were mixed. I felt sorry for the mother but was excited to get a new "pet."

Jack would walk to the other side of the car, open the door, reaching across the back seat to pull the new calf into the car and across the seat. I would then join him from the other side. With both of us holding this bleating calf and Daddy still talking to Uncle Emmitt outside the car, it was all we could do to hold the poor thing still. But hold it still we did. With Jack wrapping an arm around its neck and me with both arms around its torso, there was no way it was going to get loose.

"Come on, Daddy." Jack would say, to no one's listening ears but mine. "Is he going to stand out there and talk forever? This da-gone bull is gonna start raising Cain any minute!"

"Bla-a-a-a-a-a-a!... Bla-a-a-a-a-a!... Bla-a-a-a-a-a!..." It sounded out. The noise inside the Chevy Impala was deafening, stinging our little ears. It wanted no part of that car's backseat, or of us.

Finally, Daddy would arrive. I guess he and his older brother Emmett had run out of things to laugh at. And boy, could those two laugh. He took his place at the driver's seat and cranked up the car. Looking back at us, he'd remark, "You boys ok? You got him, right? Don't let go, whatever you do."

Daddy wheeled the big sedan in reverse over the grassy back yard, then forward onto the dirt road that led to and from the dairy barn. Dust flew away, making our way to the un-marked road fronting the house. Looking both ways and we were off.

I looked at Jack. He had that worried look that only he and I knew oh so well. Whenever we were with Daddy, we knew to be on our best behavior, do what he said, and don't screw up. In this case, "screwing up" meant doing anything that would allow that calf to break loose from our grip, damage the upholstery or, God forbid, break out a car window.

We knew to hold on tight. Daddy and we had covered all possibilities in the event something went wrong. We thought.

We were no more than a mile or two from Uncle Emmitt's when it happened. And, of course, I would have to be the one on the "wrong end of things" when it did.

The calf became strangely quiet. We had both windows down in the back seat, of course. Remember Daddy didn't believe in cars with air conditioning. The wind was whipping up pretty good, and we must have made a really strange looking pair that day, what with fine, little calf hairs swirling in the car's interior, Daddy with one elbow out the window and one hand on the steering. Jack allowed the calf to protrude its head ever so slightly out his side's car window.

Suddenly, the calf raised its tail, and I knew immediately what was about to happen. Having dealt with calves before, we had always been lucky in this department, but today it wasn't to be.

Manure quickly began to drop from the calf's backside. Jack yelled out, "Watch out!" I yelled out, "Oh shoot!" Believe me, if not for Daddy's presence, I would have chosen another word. As the stuff began to get all over me and the car, I tried with all my might to push the calf's ass out the window so at least some of the rotten, disgusting stuff could be dropped outside the car. Jack pushed from the head, and I pulled from the end. There were all sorts of moaning and crying out with disgust. The manure was runny and like no odor we had ever smelled. It was on the seat, in the floorboard, on the door, the window and all over the outside of the car. And on us.

And through all this, Daddy never stopped. Here we were two pre-teen knuckleheads holding onto this calf in the back seat of a sedan like we were on a double-date, and it crapping all over us! I wanted to cry. I think Jack did too. And just when we thought it was finished, here came more.

Jack and I held our noses as best we could while maintaining control over the calf. It continued to bleat loudly, and we were quick to join it. All three of us were desperate and miserable. And through it all, Daddy continued to just keep driving. Was the man completely outside his mind!!!???!!!

This had to be the longest ten to fifteen miles I had ever traveled in a car. No amount of fresh air from the windows or trying to ignore what we were experiencing helped. We were at the mercy of a four-legged, one-hundred+ pound animal with diarrhea and a large man who could not have cared less about our plight or about the smell emanating from the back seat. What in God's name must the man have smelled in his lifetime that would permit him to tolerate this!!??!!

We pulled into the back yard. Daddy quickly exited the front and opened my door. Daddy had a look of surprise; "Good grief, he messed all over the place" was his comment.

"No kidding, Sherlock?" I thought to myself. (No way was I going to actually SAY that.) I stepped out of the car, just past

Daddy *(Captain Obvious)* and for the first time saw myself from head to toe. My eyes bulged with shock.

"Oh my gosh!" I exclaimed. Of course, manure was on my hands, so now it was on my face too. Daddy pulled the calf out of the car and led it away to the barn's stall. Jack exited the other side, realizing it was all over him as well.

We ran over to the hose and began to strip down. Hosing ourselves off was a cold, yet very relieving experience. The entire co-ed population of Auburn Elementary could have walked up on us. I didn't care.

"God, I can't believe that dumb-ass cow did that all over us." Jack said. "Why can't we just buy meat at the grocery store like everybody else?"

"What?" I angrily thought to myself. "And miss all this fun!"

––––––––––––––––––––

Raising a calf that is not fully weaned is another story altogether. For about six to eight weeks, Jack's and my daily routine would be as such:

5:30 AM   Wake up, slip on bedroom shoes and overcoats. Gloves if really cold. Walk onto the back porch and pour two large scoops of milk powder concentrate into a bucket. Add two gallons of warm water and stir. (Keep in mind this wasn't just any bucket, but a five-gallon aluminum bucket with a large six-inch rubber nipple extended from its side near the bottom.)
5:45 AM   Walk with said bucket (in the dark) across the back yard, both carrying it so as not to spill.) Place bucket on the ground, work our way through the barbed-wire fence and begin to search for the new calf, which was not easy, since he had not yet learned what wonderful treat awaited him and that hiding in the back pasture was a fun thing to do.
6:00 AM   Finally, discover the calf some two- or three-hundred yards from the milk and do our "tail-and-ear" tugging thing to get him to the milk bucket.
6:30 AM   Coax the calf to the fence. Jack holds his head. I insert the nipple, and we both manually work the calf's mouth up

and down to get him to take the milk. Usually, after one or two squirts, he would get the idea, and the rest was relatively easy, except the part about holding this very heavy bucket in the dead of winter, or having to do all this in a driving rainstorm.

Usually, by 7:00 a.m., this dreaded chore would be over. It would take about a week of this routine, before the calf finally wised up and would be awaiting us at the pasture's edge. This meant an extra thirty minutes of sleep, as we would no longer have to walk through our pasture in search of dumb-dumb.

So, it wasn't enough that the thing crapped on us in the back seat of the car, but we had to chase it down, pull it across the pasture to the barn, and teach it how to suck!

To this day, I still can't believe we actually did this.

When the calf was finally weaned and we didn't have to "nurse" it any more, they actually became an animal that provided a little fun. From about two months to six months old, calves were the perfect size for riding, though never for long. One of us would hold the animal still, while the other climbed on board. He'd buck and run and jump all round, leaving us in a pile of grass laughing and whooping. They were the means to our own little personal rodeo. If we happened to have one of Daddy's old fedoras, it would be our make shift cowboy hat, waving it in the air with one hand while holding onto a fistful of hairy neck.

I always dreamed of maybe having a calf that would allow me to ride it like a horse, but it was never to be. Calves were never meant to be horses.

"You can't eat a horse!" Daddy would say curtly. "All they do is cost money. Besides, it'd probably get out and get run-over, and then we'd have to pay somebody for the damages." He had obviously already thought the whole thing out. So, most of my youth I would dream of horses, guns, and Indians, and my little mind would race with imaginative adventures involving all three. A stick-horse would have to do.

For most of a year, that calf would be our pet. We would literally pet it, lie in the grass with it, and even on occasion groom it. We gave all our calves a name, and each one would take on its very unique personality. There was Gaylord and Ruffy and Bart and Bret (after the Maverick brothers). And, finally there was Buck, a bull that lives still today in infamy.

Buck grew to be a very large Hereford. Daddy probably kept him alive longer than he should have, as the bigger he became, the meaner he got. Neither Jack nor I could step inside the fence, that Buck would spy us and begin running at us, head down, blowing and snorting. We always planned our trips around the pasture, with as little time INSIDE the fence as possible. Old Buck would stop just short of the fence and begin to paw the ground. I'm convinced to this day he would have killed us, given half the chance.

As long as Buck was around, we'd walk *around* the pasture, *outside* the fence, to arrive at our favorite fishing pond owned by neighbor and friend Lowell Wheeler. Wheeler's Pond was filled with bream, catfish and bass. Many a spring and summer afternoon was spent wetting a hook in that pond. Though not much bigger than an acre, it provided us with lots and lots of fun – both fishing and skinny-dipping.

One particular afternoon, after fishing alone at Wheeler's Lake, I was headed back home. With my rod-and-reel slung over my shoulders and a stringer of bream and catfish, I was extra excited about "bringing home dinner." It was a great day anytime I had good luck with my old Johnson rod-and-reel.

I hopped over the back fence of our pasture and began to cross the field, making my way toward home. Nothing was on my mind except showing off my catch to Mama. I remember it like yesterday as being a beautiful day too. Huge cumulus clouds drifted overhead, foregrounding a gorgeous blue sky. Buzzards and crows sang out overhead. I was whistling the theme song from "The Rifleman" and thinking about nothing but how much heaven must be something like this.

I wore my favorite white T-shirt, the one that now had only *one* hole in the left underarm, unlike most of my others, and easily the most comfortable T in the drawer. My blue jeans were dirty from sitting on the lake-dock and nearby dam. There were grass stains on the knees, and the faint smell of cow manure drifted up from my backside. Mr. Wheeler was a cattleman himself, so fishing meant cows, and cows meant, "watch where you're stepping. And sitting." My footwear was a pair of white *Chuck Taylor's*. They were stained as well, with the left one displaying a hole or two and the right one with shoestrings which had broken long before, only to be tied back together two or three times. An old brown belt held my jeans up. It had belonged to Jack at one time, and its end hung almost to my knees. I was a sight, but fashion was the last thing on my mind whenever fishing or play were involved.

After topping the hill in the back of the pasture, I could see the house in the distance. Mother would be in the kitchen, going through the cabinets and fridge in search of "what's for supper." It would make her day, I thought, to see me step inside the kitchen and present my catch.

"Hooray for Davey!" she'd shout. "My supper worries are over! He has saved the day again!" I could think up some real doozies when it came to my contributing to the family welfare.

Our pasture was filled with green fescue grass and plentiful patches of waist-high wheat-grass, golden rod and clover. It made a great place to play ball, hide-and-seek or fight the Civil War, all of which we did. The old terrace rows were still present from gardens and fields planted years previous. Those rows served as great defenses against approaching Yankees, defended by yours truly with my trusty hickory limb, broken and shaped to look like an 1865 carbine. I called her "Betsy." I even had a blanket roll that was part of my uniform, draped across my right shoulder and tied along the opposite side waist. Rebel yells were plentiful in 1961, and not once did old Grant or Sherman successfully breach the Brooks property. We were safe as long as I stood watch.

The pasture always seemed like the most innocent and safest of places. I loved to spend my time barefoot, jumping from one patch of clover to another, its coolness like a drug to my hot, sore feet. Nothing could put me in danger as long as I stepped onto the "Brooks farm" as I called it. Nothing, that is, except old Buck.

I was a good fifty yards from the fence line nearest our back yard when I saw him. He had been grazing to one side just below some overhanging tea olive trees. The same trees where Jack and I had played Tarzan years earlier...and I mean REALLY played Tarzan, loincloths and all. To say we were "swinging freely" had a double meaning whenever we were kings of the jungle.

Buck had been watching me the entire time, probably puzzled by the fact that I was even in his territory. As I peeked over to my right, I saw him. Suddenly, I realized what I had done. His huge black eyes caught my every move. I froze. "Oh my God. What have I done?" I thought. As quickly as I had seen him, and him me, I tossed my fishing pole to one side, and my tackle box and fish-filled stringer to the other. With a huge leap, I was off. Headed for home. So was Buck, but home wasn't what was on his mind. He had my rear end plainly in his sights. I was dead meat.

Screaming and yelling like a banshee. I didn't know who or what banshees were, but I knew they were loud. My legs couldn't churn fast enough. The grass was higher than usual, having not been cut in several months. With each kick, tuffs of straw grass flew about. I looked back only to see Buck gaining ground. It was praying time.

I've heard people say that in order to pray correctly, you should be in a proper stance, or kneel, in order to really reach God. Sorry, God, but there was no time for kneeling now!

I considered dropping to the ground and playing dead. Why not?...I was about to be just that, anyway.

Buck was snorting and pounding the ground. I know, because I could plainly hear him. It seemed as though the earth was shaking below me, partly from my own racing feet, but mostly from the one thousand pounder at my heels.

My nonsensical shouting continued. "Oh God! Oh God! Oh my God! Oh no! Oh no!" I repeated over and over, while trying to catch my breath to provide my body enough fuel for the maximum motoring speed to escape my tormentor.

Some twenty yards from the fence now, I felt Buck's slimy nostril touch the heel of one shoe. We were like two thorough-breds coming down the homestretch, except for the fact that one of the horses was screaming like a little girl. Closing in on safety, I remember stepping in cow manure, but I didn't care. Besides, stepping or falling in cow manure was something I had done often. It was not a big deal even if I had NOT been running for my life.

The side of Buck's head scraped the ankle of my other leg. I looked down and could see his terrible horns shining up at me. Daddy had sawed them off to about three inches some weeks before, but they still posed a menacing sight to a ten-year-old. His eyes were glaring up at me as he set himself on his target – the backside of my new Levi's.

"NO, BUCK! NO! NO! NO! NO! DON'T DO IT, BUCK! DON'T DO IT! NO! NO! PLEASE NO!"

I was crying out in fear. My heart was racing so that I could feel it pounding in my chest. The fence was only a few steps away. Daddy's fence posts weren't the best in the world – mostly hewn by hand, oddly shaped with three or four sides, standing erect some four-to-five feet above ground. They were quite old and some were rotting. Our wire fences were the netted type along their bottom, topped by two rows of barbed wire.

There was no time to stop to work my way through the fence. So I did my best attempt at a reverse, triple-loop, half gainer, diving head first over the fence – something I didn't know I could even attempt, but attempt I did. I was practically clear of the top rung, when my left knee caught one of the rusty, old barbs. It tore a three-inch hole down the side of my pants leg but thankfully, didn't stop me from clearing the fence, rolling into the sweet clover of the back yard and tumbling to safety. I was alive.

Turning over on my butt, knees bent, I raised my head, balancing my upper body with straight and shaken arms. I was still breathing hard. No more tears, but sweet relief came over me. I peered across the fence at Buck, who had stopped at the pasture's edge. He was standing there looking at me as if to say, "Don't you ever come into my pasture again. Next time buddy, *NO* escape."

His head was still low. He was breathing hard as well, but no snorting or puffing this time. He realized there was no way he was going to get me today. Slowly wheeling, he turned and strolled away, his tail swishing side-to-side like a clock's pendulum. I realized that a nice, smooth, egg-sized rock was resting underneath one hand. Sitting upright more, I gave it my best Yogi Berra-to-second base throw.

"YOU DUMB BASTARD! YOU ALMOST KILLED ME!...I HATE YOU! I HATE YOU! YOU HEAR?...THAT'S

OKAY... A FEW MORE MONTHS AND YOU'LL BE ON MY DINNER TABLE! YOU BUTTHEAD!...I'M GONNA ENJOY EATING YOU, YOU STUPID IDIOT!"

The rock landed hard, with a loud "POP!" directly on Buck's protruding hipbone.

"Out! At second base!" I shouted.

He turned ever so slightly, giving me a cursory look, and most assuredly thinking, "You might be okay today, but in the future, stay out of my pasture."

Our first freeze couldn't come early enough. For whenever we had livestock, cold weather meant we could harvest a bull. It was well into November that the day came when we would slaughter Buck.

I'll save you the gruesome details, but just know this: for one day every year or two, my Dad, Jack and I became executioner, castrator, veterinary surgeon, butcher and gut-hauler. A college anatomy course could never equal what we learned from butchering the family bull.

Looking back now, how strange it was to spend the greater part of a year with the family "pet," only to lead him to the big limb of the old pecan tree, where "swinging" took on a whole new meaning.

~ 16 ~
You Smell So Sweet!

Her name was Dorian. Growing up, I thought nothing of the unusual nature of the name. I had never heard anyone else with the name, but she would not have been who she was by any other name.

She was the third child of Joe and Nina. Jet black hair. A beautiful smile, and just as gorgeous a personality. She loved life, and everything she did exemplified that fact. Her smile, laugh and overall personality were contagious. She was my beauty queen sister. I was the brother of someone famous, or so I thought.

Dorian and Karen occupied the "back bedroom." They shared a double bed whose sides were no more than eight inches from the doorway and side wall. A dresser and chest of drawers took up the rest of the room.

Away from home and staying with Marilyn once, I wrote a letter home and explained to Mama that I had "put up all my clothes in Marilyn's *chester draws*. What do you expect? That's the way I had always heard it.

Dorian was the prissy sister, and Karen seemed like "one of the guys." Whenever they'd fight or have an argument, it meant splitting up the bedroom, with each one possessing a side. Funny now, considering the room's size: bottom line, each one owned four square feet. The entry way was a neutral zone.

They would create a "DMZ line," that the other was not to

cross. Invariably, I'd come into their room and the shouting would begin, "Get out of my side!" one would shout. So I'd cross over only to hear the other one exclaim, "Get off my side too!" It would be so confusing; I'd just jump onto the bed, only to hear them shouting more, since they had divided that up too. I'd leap from the bed out the door and into the safe zone of the hallway. "Girls!" I'd shout, in utter disgust.

They were true teenagers of the 50s. Saddle oxfords and bobby socks, ponytails, poodle skirts, high waisted pedal pushers, blouses with round "Peter-Pan" collars and perfume. Ah the perfume. You couldn't walk into their bedroom without the smell immediately permeating the room. If you took Mama's rose garden, her petunias and lilacs and combined them with the sweet fragrances of her cakes and pies, ah yes, that was the smell of Dorian and Karen's perfumes.

As a four- and five-year-old, I was a curious little cuss. I loved adventuring throughout the house on cold or rainy days. Sandra was married. Marilyn was away at nursing school, Dorian and Karen were in high school, and Jack was doing his thing at Auburn Elementary. It was just Mama and me.

I made tunnels by turning the dining chairs upside down and lining them up. I crawled under everyone's bed in search of a loose sock, ball or toy. I climbed up the chifferobe, that I called the "shift-a-robe," by pulling out each drawer just so far and stepping up its front to the top. From there, I could see everything in the room from a bird's-eye-view. It made me feel as tall as Daddy.

I loved going into Dorian and Karen's room. Since they weren't there to yell me out, I had the run of the space. Sweet! Under their bed was a great place. I loved the cool wooden floor against my face and hands. Not to mention the neat hair pins, ribbons, scarves and hair bands that could be found there. Scarves were perfect for "cowboying," and hairpins made a neat musical instrument. Ribbons could be tied to my stick horse and used as reins.

Still to this day, there is no trampoline as fun as the bounce you could get from a good old double bed. I could almost touch the ceiling. On rainy days, I'd open the windows and smell the fresh scent of falling spring water. If raining hard enough, water would gather on the window screen, filling each one of the tiny screen-squares. Putting my mouth against the screen and sucking meant a cold, wet treat of fresh rain and cool air.

I loved sitting on the side of the bed, pressing my face against the screen and waiting for the big yellow school bus that would return Dorian and Karen home each day. I knew the exact time it would appear in the distance, rolling westward from Winder. As soon as it would appear, I'd run through the hallway, Aunt Ruby's room, the den, living room and front porch to greet them as they walked across the road from the waiting bus. I was like the little puppy whose bigger siblings were returning to the litter. Bouncing around, smiling and laughing, and wondering what treat they might have brought home.

The drawers where Dorian kept her things were like opening buried treasure. She must have owned a hundred scarves. Enough to allow me to be color coordinated with my shirt and pants, if I had wanted to be. Sometimes I could find some Juicy Fruit gum or a Hershey's Kiss. "She wouldn't miss them." I'd think. She had pencils, erasers, more hairpins and girly stuff, a few pennies (for the tracks), pictures of her friends at school, some dumb letter from another girl, a keychain or two, and jewelry.

On top of her dresser was always a doily that either Mom or Aunt Ruby had made, a lamp and a few things she owned, like her perfume.

The day before, Dorian had been given, what was to be a very precious gift.

Dorian's boyfriend at the time was a young man named Nick. He and Dorian went everywhere together. At least everywhere in tiny Barrow County. They were in love, if you can call it that at such a young age. Nick's mother worked at the local Winder Pharmacy, and she had helped him pick out a special bottle of perfume as a gift to Dorian. Her very first bottle of perfume, it turns out. It was tenderly wrapped with beautiful pink satin paper and matching bow.

Dorian was so excited she carefully placed it in a special place of honor on her bedroom dresser. It was to be used sparingly. She thought.

It probably came from the Herrin's Drugstore in Winder and must have cost quite a lot for the times. Herrin's sat directly next door to Roses five-and-dime on Winder's Broad Street. *The* place to be on any given Saturday morning, while Mom did her regular weekly shopping.

Dorian spent a short time working at Rose's, when she was in High School. I doubt she made twenty-five cents an hour. On Saturdays, when I'd go to town with Mom, I'd stroll into Roses and spy her behind the candy counter. She'd see me staring at all the wonderful treats through the glass enclosures and ask, "How much money do you have?" To which I'd reach in my pockets and pull out four cents. Showing it to her, she'd weigh out four cents of cashews, slide them into a bag and hand them across the counter. Four cents didn't buy much, but it was a great treat nonetheless. This little move was known as the "Brooks scam," an inside job intended to rid Rose's of as many cashews as possible.

Actually, it was just a simple act of kindness by a sister who loved me. Still to this day, I'm hooked on cashews.

Thanks, Dorian.

I loved to pick up the various bottles and spray cans resting on her dresser. Hair spray was like Flash Gordon's laser gun intended to kill Martian flies. Bath soaps were cool drawing tools on their mirror. Lipstick too. I had seen them putting this crazy stuff on their lips. Why not? Plus, red was a great color for a Pirate tattoo – usually a big heart with "Mother" written across it – something any self-respecting Pirate would have. Her scarves made a great headpiece, and a careful placement of one earbob topped off the ensemble. "Arrrrgggghhh."

Safety pins and hairpins could be linked together to make a great necklace, and the cardboard piece from a wire coat hanger served as the perfect sword. Everywhere I looked in their room, there appeared another costume piece, ready for the taking. With a little imagination, I could "dress up" just like a character right out of central casting.

I spied Dorian's cherished perfume on her dresser. Something this small, containing such a small amount of "colored" water must be pretty special. Especially given the fact that it sat all by itself in the center of the dresser, just waiting for a pair of prying hands to investigate. It had the neatest top on it too, a round cut-glass screw top that resembled a tiny doorknob. Ah! So this is where the secret smell is coming from!

I had seen Dorian that morning dab a little bit of this magical elixir under her ears, being careful only to put one finger on its tip, turning it upside down. This looked really curious, except she wasn't using very much of the stuff. I was certain that one was supposed to use more that THAT! Besides, putting it behind her ears was a dumb thing to do.

I stared at the bottle top. Placing my face just in front of it, I could see my reflection on each of the finely cut edges. There were at least ten of me staring back. I slid the bottle closer to me, and slowly unscrewed the top. Carefully placing the lid to one side, I tilted the bottle toward my curious nose and took a huge sniff of its sweet aroma. Wow! This stuff smells better than Dale Evans must have smelled the first time she met Roy. (Or perhaps, it was how Roy smelled!) No wonder Roy was so hot for her! And I thought it was her cool horse, Buttermilk, that attracted the King of the Cowboys!

My next move was to try her "finger-tip-behind-the-ears" move I had witnessed. After all, maybe I could attract a horse-riding gal as cute as Dale.

Didn't do much for me.

There's no way this is going to make any difference in my magnetism. After all, if I'm gonna be the King of the Cowboys, it's gonna take a whole lot more than a couple of finger-dabs behind the ears!

With that logic, I turned the bottle upside down and began to splash large amounts into my palms, patting it on my face – like a real MAN!...something I had seen Daddy do with his Old Spice after shave. Still not enough.

Okay, let's rub a little onto my underarms. Saw that once too. Then a little more on my shoes; maybe I wouldn't have to wash my feet tonight! And, of course, I can't forget my hair. When I bow to greet a new suitor, they might get a good whiff of my head and faint from the pleasantness.

Finally, I was there. A walking, talking bottle of "whatever that stuff was on Dorian's dresser." I was totally convinced that whomever I encountered, they would be completely pleased and overwhelmed by my scent. I must have smelled something like a Hollywood hooker.

About that time, I heard the loud squealing of the brakes of a school bus out front – an unmistakable sound to a four-year-old anticipating the return of his siblings. Doing my usual running-through-the-house thing, I leaped out the front door to await my Princesses returning from school. Dorian was the first to cross the highway. Jumping onto the sidewalk with her books resting firmly under her arms, her smile seemed as broad as ever. She quickly and carefully placed her books on the sidewalk and rose to find me jumping into her arms.

"Dorian!" I shouted. "You're home!" Karen joined our hug to one side. What a joy it was to be greeted each day by two sisters I loved so much.

"Davey!" Dorian cried, hugging me with all her might. "My goodness, you smell sooooo sweeeeet!" she shouted innocently. Looking over her shoulder, I could see some of the kids on the bus as it pulled away, staring at our reunion. "Look at me," I thought. "See how important I am to these girls!"

"I don't think I've ever smelled anything so sweet!" she repeated.

"You are just so, so, . . ." Then, just as suddenly, her expression and entire demeanor changed. From pure delight to unadulterated terror.

I'm certain that several images abruptly entered Dorian's head:

Her FIRST bottle of perfume. Her first gift from a boy. Her carefully bringing it home and finding that special spot on her dresser for it to occupy. Her ever so slowly using drop by drop so as to make it last as long as possible... Her baby brother, whom she loved so much, about to be murdered.

"AHHHHHHHHHHHH!!!!...Tell me you didn't!" she cried. "NO, NO, NO!...OH NO!. . . YOU DIDN'T."

What the heck was she so all fired upset about? She tossed me into the grass and ran into the house. Obviously, she was excited for me that I had found her smelly stuff and used it.

Not quite.

I sat in the grass and could hear her every step through the house on her way to her room. Then, another yell, only three times the volume of the previous, "AHHHHHHHHHHHHH!!!"

Up until that day, I had never seen Dorian cry. That day, she cried.

Eventually, some years later, Dorian got over it. I think it might have been thirty or forty years later. And for at least several weeks after my little perfume caper, Dorian and Karen's room was 'off-limits' to this little curious cuss.

What was the big deal, I wondered. She could easily replace it by pouring some of Daddy's Old Spice into that little bottle. None the worse for wear.

One of these days, I've got to buy that sweet girl some perfume…and it better be some really good stuff.

Definitely not Old Spice.

~ 17 ~
Go Back and Cut It Again

Karen was five years older than Jack and eight years my senior. She was incredibly sweet when she wanted to be. But when she decided to be angry, look out. No taller than a wisp, she towered over us, as youngsters. She played basketball with us, drove us places once she reached driving age, kept us away from the television if "Bandstand" or "Armchair Playhouse" were on, and taught us how to play Solitaire and Rummy.

One of my keenest memories was growing old enough and big enough to cut the grass. Up until age eight, cutting grass had been a chore for Karen and Jack. Karen cut the large open areas of our yard and Jack cut around the house where the ever-present trees, flowers and shrubs made grass-cutting like a tortuous maze.

The day finally arrived that I was to join the "crew" in cutting the grass, pulling weeds or laying rocks around things. Our sweet Aunt Ruby would often say, "If you don't behave, you're going to wind up on the rock pile." I was never certain as to what exactly that meant, until years later observing some old Humphrey Bogart movie with hoards of sweaty, dirty men wearing striped pajamas and slaving away at piles of rock, pick-axes in hand.

I was up early. It was a Saturday, I'm sure. The old gray Craftsman push mower was always stowed away under the back porch together with stacks of wood, an old kitchen cabinet, tools, the wheelbarrow and anything else that we thought might fit there.

The space was so dark and dusty. There wasn't one blade of grass. Rather just dirt: a nice mix of white sand, red clay and cobwebs. I despised the place. You couldn't walk into the area without exiting with spider- and cobwebs covering various parts of your body. I can't help but be reminded of that area of the house every time I see someone decorating their house for Halloween, replete with store-bought cobwebs. If I only knew: I could have collected enough of the stuff over the years to be set for life. Dave's cobwebs. $1.99 a bag. Get'em while they're hot!

Another hot summer, 1959. If the lawn mower wasn't pushed all the way under the shaded porch, and the handles were left out in the scorching sun, it would be hot to the touch. The mower's handles had long lost their vinyl covers, leaving only the metal rods for gripping. Quickly grasping the handles let you know real quick just how hot. Karen and Jack stood off to the side as I grabbed hold of the handles. "Ow-ee! Ow-ee! Ooooh! Ouch!" as I pulled the mower from under its dank home. Touch. Release. Touch Release. Man, was it hot. How in the blue blazes was I supposed to cut grass with the handles so hot? Jack checked the gas, as Karen walked over to the water hose. A quick dowsing of the handles and we were almost ready.

The mower's pull-rope hung dangling from the handles. Karen untied it and slowly set the knot in the starter's groove and wrapped it around four or five times. With a quick pull, the mower stuttered with a loud muffled groan, but alas did not start.

"Now. That's the way you start up the thing, so you try it." She said. This was so cool. I was about to step into manhood by showing everyone how strong I was by starting up the mower all by myself. Setting the knot, I followed Karen's example, slowly wrapping it around the starter. Setting my left foot on the side of the mower, I held the rope handle with both hands and steadied myself. I was ready. Counting to three in my head, I gave a monstrous pull, utilizing every little muscle in my frame. I whipped my entire sixty-five pounds up into the air with a mighty flourish. The handle slipped right out of my hands, clanging against various mower parts, as I was thrown back by my own exertion, landing with a thunderous "ker-thud!" right onto my scrawny little back side.

Karen and Jack were whooping it up. No episode of "The Three Stooges" could have been funnier to them. Jack fell back on his rump with laughter, as Karen was slapping a knee, doing her best impression of me attempting the seemingly impossible. I dusted myself off, red-faced and somewhat ashamed that the starter had not turned one bit. "Let me try." Jack said. Going through the same gyrations, he had the same results, except that the mower almost started, and he wasn't lying on the grass in embarrassment. A couple of more tries resulted in the same. Even Karen couldn't get it started. I noticed that both of them kept fiddling with a small lever just below the crankcase each time they would make their attempt. "What's that?" I asked.

"It's the choke, silly." It's how you start the engine. It allows extra gas to get into the engine. We may have flooded it though." "Flooded it?" I thought. I looked around for standing water. It hadn't rained in weeks. How could it possibly be flooded?

This routine went on for some time, until the old thing finally started. I had never stood this close to a running mower. The noise was deafening, I thought, and the smoke parting from the muffler was blinding. Seeing all the smoke, Karen remarked that indeed we had almost flooded the engine. Again, there was no sign of rain.

She next began to demonstrate how best to cut grass. In nice straight rows, making sure the wheels ever so slightly overlapped the previous cut row. I looked up at Jack. He was rolling his eyes, as if he had heard this speech at least a dozen times before. Indeed he had. This whole experience was new to me, however, so I made sure to listen carefully.

After cutting two or three rows, Karen put the mower in front of me, "There you go, little buddy. Have at it." The end of the handle was about three inches below my eyes. Reaching out with both hands, I took hold of the "reins" and began to "push my horse." Except that the mower was more like a stubborn mule.

Somehow, it wasn't quite as easy as Jack and Karen had made it seem. I immediately realized that, in order to push the mower along the back yard, I had to lean into it. And I mean really lean into it. With arms outstretched, head down and my legs extended for leverage, it was all I could do to propel the darn thing across our yard. The space between the mower and my feet was wide enough for a large go-kart to drive under. Sweat quickly formed over my brow, as the Craftsman became heavier and heavier. Coming to the end of the yard near the pasture fence, I quickly turned it around and began my long trek back in the direction of the house and my awaiting supervisor, Karen. I remembered how she had told me to overlap the rows just a bit in order to cover the entire yard, but in my effort just to stay upright and mobile, where I was along the row took a backseat to my ability to propel the old mule. Stopping right in front of Karen, I looked up at her, and then back at the two rows I had so dutifully mowed. Those two rows were a thing of beauty.

Karen took one look at them and began to march out the yard pointing out every little blade of grass I had missed. "Here!...and here!...and here's another one…and here too!"

This girl was the grass-Nazi. I couldn't believe what she was saying. "Go back and cut it again" were the words that escaped her lips. She was not happy.

"Was it really all that important?" I asked.

She just rolled her eyes and repeated those awful words, "Go back and cut it again!"

So back I went. Over the same ground I had just covered. Jack stood aside snickering at this entire turn of events. It entered my mind that he probably had been over the same scenario as I, some years earlier. So cut it again I did. We must have repeated this same routine nine or ten times, until at last the yard was cut…or at least that portion that Jack (and now I) was responsible for.

I recall most of the years that Karen lived at home. She was eighteen when she moved away to Georgia Baptist Nursing School in Atlanta. Following our older sister's footsteps, she longed to be a nurse, to take care of others, to be like Marilyn.

Karen was a fairly accomplished pianist as well. At least in comparison to her five siblings. All of Joe and Nina's children, at one time or another took piano lessons. But it was only Karen and Sandra who turned out to be the siblings who could get by as a piano player.

Some years after her marriage to Charles Henderson of Griffin, Georgia, they purchased their first home in Conyers, Georgia. Karen had finally acquired the space to have our upright piano moved out of the house in Carl and off to Conyers.

With Dad's truck parked in the right lane of Highway 29 in front of our house, we carefully rolled the monstrosity out the front door and up the front walkway. It might just as well have weighed ten thousand pounds. With two teenaged boys, Jack and me, and Pops as moving men, we pulled up one side of the piano and gradually settled it onto the bed of Dad's Chevy pickup. All three of us stood behind and with everything we could muster, we lifted the other side and fully onto the truck. Moaning and groaning were definitely in excess that afternoon. Karen gently set the piano bench onto the truck, just in front of the piano.

Dad entered the cab, rested himself behind the steering wheel and cranked her up.

Karen couldn't resist. She jumped into the truck bed, slid across the piano bench and raised the keyboard cover. As Dad slowly began to pull away for the trip from Carl to Conyers, not realizing that Karen had hopped on board, the sweet sounds of "Your Cheating Heart" came wafting across our ears. And Dad's. Slowly coming to a stop, Dad exited the truck. I don't think I had ever heard him laugh so hard. Mother, Jack and I just hooted. I doubt anyone had ever driven down Highway 29 in Carl with a young lady in the back of a pickup truck, playing Hank Williams tunes. It was one funny sight.

Karen had the natural ability to make people laugh. She was in many ways the family comedian. She had a great high-pitched laugh, with eyes squinted in pure delight. She was passionate about things. Especially passionate about family. About being prideful, sometimes to a fault. One of the true Brooks traits was pride. "You can mess with me, but don't mess with my children." She'd say. More than once I heard other sisters utter those same words.

Her anger could flow over at times, and begin to eat away at her, only to give way to understanding later on. She was book-smart too. An avid reader, she could speed-read through a book as fast as anyone I ever knew.

Karen was the second sibling to pass away. Suffering for years from polycystic kidney disease and an enlarged liver, she slowly dwindled away. Watching her pass on, in that Tampa hospital room was painful to witness. It reminded me of past experiences with Dad and Mom, and with our sister Sandra. Only this time, a certain sense of relief came over me, different from the other experiences. Believing as I do that there is life after death, it was a comfort to know that she was no longer in pain. Witnessing her discomfort over several years, and witnessing the pain and hardship her husband and children went through at her side, it was in many ways a relief, and at the same time a release. She breathed her last breath as her four remaining siblings stood around her, together with her husband, children and various in-laws. Tears flowed down all our cheeks as we encouraged her over to the other side. "She is finally pain-free!" I shouted as the endless beep came over the heart monitor. She had straight-lined. Straight-lined right into the arms of Mama and Daddy, her Aunt Ruby, Sandra and all the saints before her who had nursed her, loved her and made her so special to us all.

Suddenly I longed for some word from her. Some sign that everything was okay. Walking down the hall from her room, I thought of all the things she had done for me. How she had loved me unconditionally. How she had held my hand when it needed to be held. She was gone, but somehow I held onto the knowledge that I would see her again. That my spirit would recognize her spirit. That what was lying on that bed was just her shell. The physical vehicle that her spirit had dwelled within, all those years. And that a little piece of her would continue to dwell inside all those who knew her, both family and friends.

I never want to forget her voice. Her laughter. Her courageous fighting spirit.

I don't even want to forget her excessive and incessant command to "Go back and cut it again."

~ 18 ~
Through a Glass Dimly

The fact is, I will never know, really, what it was like to be Black in Barrow County, for obvious reasons: I am White.

I can only relate their experiences, and mine, as I viewed them, through young, innocent eyes, and by way of the few times we related to African-Americans . . . as a privileged White boy. Though at the time, I never realized such privilege existed.

My Daddy would have laughed at the term African-American. There was a time when I probably would have laughed too. Ignorance and prejudice are sort of like communicable diseases. They can be allowed to spread, but they can be healed. I've discovered things and grown a lot through the years. I suppose you are what you come from, but it doesn't mean you can't change, mature, and look outside yourself once in a while. It just isn't completely true that you can't take the "Carl" out of the boy. Yes, part of me will always be "Carl," but most of me will never return to that state of mind. Thomas Wolfe said it best, "You can't go home again." For some of this profound truth, I am thankful.

Depending on the decade, being Black had different meanings in Carl. During the 50s, Black people regularly kept to themselves. We would see them in their yards playing, or at the store on rare occasions.

The only contact between Whites and Blacks was

superficial, coming out of necessity. For the most part, we never socialized with one another.

The Ku Klux Klan had a presence in our community. I remember that once or twice each year they would hold a rally. I was never sure where, but the days leading up to the rally meant them driving up and down the road, speaking through a loud speaker attached to their cars announcing the upcoming event: "BIG KKK RALLY THIS SATURDAY NIGHT AT J.B. SATTERFIELD'S PASTURE! COME ONE, COME ALL! HELP US STAMP OUT THE BLACK RACE! NEGROES AND JEWS NOT WELCOME..!" and on and on.

My cousin Mark and I were playing football in the side yard of our house when I remember them appearing along Highway 29. We both froze in our tracks to watch and listen with much curiosity. But I remember a chill running up my spine as they appeared. In some ways, it was very confusing to be taught love at church, at home and at school, and then listen to the preaching of hate that was allowed to pervade our little town. I supposed that it was okay to NOT love, as long as it involved people somehow different from us.

The n-word was used regularly. I heard Daddy use it. I heard my friends use it. I even heard my preacher use it. Yes, even I used it, though rarely, and am ashamed today to admit it. It wasn't much of an excuse, but we just didn't know any better. It was in many ways, all we knew. It was out of ignorance and fear that we related to African-Americans in our community. They were "different." They went to different schools. They sat in the balcony of the local theatre in Winder. They drank from separate water fountains. When the County Fair came to Winder, even a day was set aside for only Blacks to attend. It was called "n-----day." (I even find it hard to write the word or think about its past/current usages today.) Blacks were seen in Winder at the local stores with their heads held low, very inconspicuous. Almost like they were ashamed "to be." I know now it was out of fear. They were to be seen, not heard. Tolerated, though shunned.

How sad. How utterly sinful.

I had only one acquaintance growing up who was Black. His name was "Popcorn." That's all. No first or last name. Just

Popcorn. I'm not sure how or why anyone came up with that name, but Popcorn was who he was – named so by the Black and White communities alike. I would meet up with him in the woods far behind our property. We'd play chase or hide-and-seek or 1-2-3 red light. Those were fun, innocent days, as long as we kept to ourselves, and no one knew of our play together. When 4:45 PM came each day, I'd turn to head for home, as would he, and our lives would continue very much separate.

I remember seeing him with tattered, worn clothes. His shirt usually had several holes in it, as well as his jeans. Like us, he was barefooted most of the time, and he, like us, smelled due to hours of sweat from non-stop, roughshod play. His hair was somewhat matted, and his feet were always dirty. I was curious to discover his feet and palms were the same color as mine. Looking back on him now, except for his skin color, he was just like us. Simply a kid who wanted to have friends and make life as fun as possible. In those early years, I never knew his real name. As before, not knowing his last name was in itself a commentary of Black/White relations in the 1950s and 60s.

There was another Black man, much older, in the Auburn/Carl area. We would frequently see him riding a green farm wagon being pulled by one or two mules. He would make his way up and down Highway 29, off on some errand for Mr. Bob Hargrove. Mr. Hargrove was the storeowner in Auburn who probably had more land and farm animals than anyone else. The old Black man who seemed to be doubling as Bob's man-Friday was named "Tobe," pronounced like 'robe."

We called him Mr. Tobe to his face, or Old Tobe, when not in his presence. Mr. Tobe was probably no more than fifty years old, but his mannerisms and countenance said he was a good bit older. He walked with a stoop, sometimes using a cane. He always wore overalls – torn and soiled. His undershirt was just that, a long-sleeved undershirt or "long-john shirt," white, but also a bit worn and torn. His hair was snow white, deeply matted and uncombed. He was for the most part unkempt and odorous, but his disposition was kind. I know from witnessing him that he was hard working, and probably paid very little, as were most Blacks in rural Georgia at that time. Old Tobe could usually be found wearing a large fedora-style straw hat; of course, it too was torn and overused.

The wagon, the mules, Tobe's home and the very land he farmed were all owned by Mr. Hargrove. On the rare occasion that Daddy had to borrow the wagon and mules for hauling things, I always thought he was borrowing from Mr. Tobe. I discovered much later that it was Mr. Hargrove doing the loaning.

Jack and I loved to ride on the back of Mr. Tobe's wagon, when we would see him out and about. What fun. We'd drag our feet off the back of the wagon's tailgate, and lean over and down to watch the ground drift by. Sometimes we'd drag our shoes a little in the loose gravel, that is until the day one of the mules decided to relieve itself, and our feet became mired in the manure.

Mr. Tobe was a kind man, who loved children, both Black and White.

Some time in the mid-1960's, desegregation hit Barrow County Schools. Up until that day, I had never seen a Black child on the bus, much less attended school with a minority child.

The first day of school came and there he was. Popcorn. Though he had grown, and I had not seen him in years, he was still very recognizable. I would later discover his name to be Charles Monroe. Charles had arrived at the Auburn school to board the bus headed east for Winder. I would discover that he lived just behind the Auburn school with Tobe. Tobe was his grandfather. There's an irony in thinking "small world" when considering Carl, Georgia. Popcorn's real name, his relationship with Tobe - all of this I could have and should have known, had I just asked. Had I been curious enough to look outward, beyond our little hamlet along the highway.

I boarded the bus headed toward Auburn where it would take on other high schoolers who used the elementary school as a pick-up point. I was ready for the first day of high school. I had on a new pair of pants, tasseled wing tips and a new *Izod* shirt. Both nervous and anxious about my first day away from my beloved Auburn Elementary, I sat with David Smith and watched as the older students boarded one by one. Looking out the right-side window, I spied Popcorn in the back of the line. He too was dressed to the nines, clearly expecting an exciting day at Winder-

Barrow. All of us kids stared at him, as if he were a Martian. We had never seen a Black student on a Barrow County "Whites-only" school campus. Slowly, the students made their way to the door of the bus with each stepping gradually upward like minnows being swallowed by a giant yellow whale.

Then, it came Charles's turn to board.

Our substitute bus driver that day, a Mr. Johnston, was a friendly man. (He often subbed for the regular drivers of Barrow County from time to time.) He would often joke with us as we entered the bus each morning and departed for home in the afternoon. He always spoke with a friendly "Good morning," or a jovial, "Have a good day." I thought him to be a friend to us all. To know him was to love him.

After Charles had made his first step and then his second onto the bus, Mr. Johnston turned in his seat to face Charles. Standing abruptly, he said in a voice I had never heard come from him, "You ain't gettin' on this bus. Step right off here, right now!"

Charles looked confused. Not knowing what to say or do, he froze, seemingly not believing what just occurred. He didn't step back or walk forward. He simply stood there. Time stood still for a moment.

"I said git off MY BUS!...NOW!" he repeated.

Never taking his eyes off Mr. Johnston, Charles back-pedaled off the bus and stood on the concrete curb. With a brave, yet somewhat meek and trembling voice, he replied, "I have a right to ride this bus. You can't keep me from riding."

The entire busload of students went stone cold silent. Charles made a motion as if to attempt to board the bus again. Mr. Johnston quickly stepped down the bus's entry way and stood defiantly in front of the door, "Nigger, you gonna board over my dead body!" He shouted, going chest-to-chest with Charles.

Charles was a very dark-skinned African-American. The whites of his eyes shone brightly, contrasting his ebony face. I could almost make out tears welling up along the bottom edge of his eyes. He was shaking. Not from fear but from sheer frustration. Perhaps anger. I leaned forward in my seat, rising a little for a better view. This was drama like I had never witnessed. A young ninth-grade student standing up to an adult for what he truly believed in. Courage and character under fire. Charles "Popcorn" Monroe was standing up for what he knew was right.

Mr. Johnston pushed Charles aside. Charles made a motion as if he would retaliate, but did not. Still more courage.

In an instant, the Auburn principal appeared, separated the two, and pulled the bus driver aside. "That nigger ain't gettin' on MY BUS!" he repeated to the principal. "They don't pay me enough to drive niggers to school!"

Even now, looking back on what happened that day, it pains me to consider the fact that I did nothing. I said nothing. I offered no words of encouragement for Charles, but my senses told me this was just dead wrong.

I could see the principal, Mr. Boston lecturing the irate bus driver. An attempt to calm the bus driver was quite evident, but it was also clear that Mr. Johnston would have nothing of it. Heated words were exchanged still further. They had reached an impasse. Still shaking and visibly upset, Charles stood to one side observing the two men. The quiet bus awaited the decision. What would come of Charles? How was he going to get to school? Was Mr. Johnston going to be fired right here on the spot? Removed from the "driver-sub" list. Were we going to make it to school ourselves?

Two buses made their way from the Auburn/Carl area to Winder-Barrow High School each day. Mr. Johnston was the "sub" driver of bus #9 that day. Mr. Campton drove #15. After a quick chat between Mr. Boston and Campton, whose bus was parked just behind old #9, they determined that Charles would ride *his* bus that day. Mr. Boston led Charles to bus #15. He boarded without so much as a whimper from Campton or the students.

Mr. Johnston got back on his bus, set the bus in gear and off we went. He jerked the bus into each gear as it entered the highway in front of the school. "Da-gone niggers! Who do they think they are? Ain't no black cat gon' ride my bus, not as long as I'm alive." He sneered and even smiled into the rear view mirror above him. I could see a real sense of victory in his facial expression. That somehow he had stood up to the U.S. government and won. That no government institution, Federal or State, was going to tell this bus driver what to do.

Our driver that day was very much a sign of the times. I dare say most adults felt the same way he did. My own Father might have reacted the same way he did, given the same circumstances. Not excusing anyone, but it was the way it was in the 1950's and 60's. *Sadly,* it was the way it was.

I kept still and quiet in my seat, as did everyone that day, all the way to Winder. Johnston continued to fume and complain. His face blood red with anger and unadulterated hatred, he had a captive audience in us. He was the preacher that day; we were his congregation. I knew better than to speak. I had witnessed first hand what happens when ignorance and fear meet common sense. I had seen anger and near violence defeat reasoning – at least for the time being. And all this from a man whom we respected and loved. A man we knew loved us. Well, most of us.

It was only a few days later that word spread: Mr. Johnston had been dressed down. Not only by Mr. Boston, but also by the County School Superintendent. I guess he wanted to keep his job, though only part time, for the next time he subbed, Charles was boarding his bus and taking his rightful seat on bus #9.

He rode that bus for the rest of the school year, and thankfully, there were no further incidences from the subs or regular drivers.

The events that year never made the paper. It wasn't on anyone's evening news. But what Charles "Popcorn" Monroe had done that day and that week was just as important and just as courageous as what Rosa Parks had done some years earlier in Montgomery, Alabama. Charles was a hero of sorts, in my mind. But I never told him, or let on that I had admired him for what he did. I was a coward to the truth. Afraid of the consequences and judgment that might come my way. Not until some years later, when things were much clearer. Much safer. And much easier.

In 2009, our class held its 40th high school reunion. My wife and I sat near the center of the old Lions Club in Winder. Having greeted most of the people I knew from those days back in Winder, we had sat down to enjoy our meal when in walked Charles. He was wearing a suit. Hair perfectly combed, he sported a goatee along with a few pounds added, like me, since 1969. I shook his hand and gave him a hug. It was my pitiful way of saying, "I'm sorry." For all those times I should have stood up for him, said something, encouraged him, and more, but did nothing.

I told him how much I admired him. How I was sorry for not befriending him in public. For turning away when he probably needed friends the most. He seemed surprised and perplexed by my words, as if my betrayal had had absolutely no effect on him. And probably it hadn't . . . only on *me.*

We chatted for a while about those crazy days in the 60s. I met his beautiful wife and he mine. They exchanged pleasantries. Charles is a lawyer now, living in Atlanta. We both had become older and heavier, and at least one thing for sure – I was wiser.

In talking about high school experiences, Charles ended our conversation with a simple statement, "You know for me, going to Winder-Barrow was just about having a new book. That's all it was, I just wanted to read and study from a new book."

I again went silent. My mouth dropped open. A look of surprise and bewilderment came over me.

"Wow." I thought. "He went through all that just to have new *books*? *NEW BOOKS!?"*

So simple, yet so very incredibly profound. I finally understood. At least partly. Yet another layer of prejudice and ignorance was swept away from my being that day. My road to perfection, though I will never arrive, became a little smoother and a little easier to tread. A little more understanding came over me. I must have stared, though briefly, at Charles, in pure amazement.

I settled back into my seat, and as a tear welled up in one eye, I gazed into my glass of tea, fingering the droplets of sweat along its side. I thought about how far I'd come. How far WE'D come. And yet, how so very much farther we still had to go.

I thought about our old home place, the year before, succumbed to a bulldozer, followed by spreading grass and weeds. (It was torn down the same week Karen passed away.)

The old train tracks came to mind. I thought about Sam and Sally. And I thought about Daddy and the prejudices he (and I) carried with us, like a weight on our very souls. Like so many chains bringing us down, all those years ago.

And, I thought about my sweet Mama. How she never allowed the n-word to be used around her. Mother, who carried a respect for all, no matter the race or religion. Mother, who loved others unconditionally. Who loved me, unconditionally.

There's that word again. *Unconditionally.* It comforts me today. Oh, if only we could *all* practice it.

Then, I heard her words echoing in my head. Words she repeated all too often during that crazy decade of the 1960s, as she stared into the television set, trying to grasp the news of yet another civil rights leader slain. "Why?" she'd whisper.

And, through her tears and fears, "Lord help us..." she'd mutter.

Yes, Mama, Lord help us, indeed.

~ ~ ~

Postscript

My parents, Aunt Ruby, four older sisters and an older brother loved me through all kinds of experiences. Always.

Sure, I was probably overly mothered, and at times the butt of jokes, but I wouldn't change a thing. We were a rag-tag bunch at times, but none of us ever missed a meal, whether at home or at school. We may not have been clean all the time, but by golly, we were clean when we were out in public. Daddy would say, "I don't care how poor you are, you can afford a bar of soap."

We were poor monetarily, but we most assuredly didn't know it. We had each other to lean on, to listen and talk to. The Brooks children were always well cared for and well educated. I don't think anyone at school, church or the other many circles we traversed could ever truthfully say we were ill behaved.

All six of us were educated beyond high school, in spite of the fact that Daddy never made over $10,000 a year. He, with only an eighth-grade education, and mother having graduated high school, both realized the importance of education early on. And they knew the importance of instilling in us the importance of earning an honest dollar to help pay most if not all of our own ways. The key to our success was to "get as much schooling as we could" before embarking on life. They instilled that in us, and we carried that importance like a badge of honor.

Another trait of us six was tolerance. Mother made sure of that. We were not to use that awful n-word. We were to be accepting of others' faults. We were to respect adults, no matter what, and we were to be thankful for the conditions in which we lived, for they were far better than so many others. She taught us that we were rich in so many ways beyond the almighty dollar. We had an intact family, extended family and friends who cared for and about us, unconditionally. We had a roof over our heads and food on the table. Who could ever want for more?

Additionally, we survived that busy highway a few steps from our front door. And the frequent clamoring of the trains, forever part of our lives.

Joe and Nina did what they were supposed to do. They loved us, provided for our needs, and helped us along our way, even into adulthood. We owe them only the responsibility of continuing the traditions of family, independence, respect and love to and for *our* descendents as well.

NOTE: As of February 2019, three Brooks children are still living. Marilyn passed away with kidney disease in October 2016, leaving Dorian as the only surviving sister. She lives with her husband Erwin at Big Canoe in Jasper, Georgia. Jack and his lovely wife Beverley live in Riverview, Florida, and recently, my wife Jane and I moved into a "fixer-upper" some three miles from Dorian, also at Big Canoe. Where there once were six, now there are three.

We still continue to vacation together, seeing one another regularly. As siblings, we've spent extended vacations together in France, Switzerland, Portugal, a European River Cruise, Myrtle Beach, Nashville, Destin, St. Simons, Las Vegas, England, Scotland, Ireland, Peru, Israel and Egypt. I'm constantly amazed at the number of people who remark about our travels together, "I can't believe you vacation with your brothers and sisters. I could never do that!"

Wherever we go, our conversations always lead us back home. Back to that little farmhouse in Carl. To Mama and Daddy and Aunt Ruby. If nothing else, those three instilled in us a yearning to stay in touch and be together as much as possible. Yet another gift representing their love for us.

And Oh, what a gift.

The author, David Allen Brooks,
can be reached at his Email: boppo1@bellsouth.net.
If possible, a Review of this book would be greatly appreciated,
by going to the book's Amazon site.
Watch for his next book, "Mind Fullness" available soon.

Made in the USA
Middletown, DE
09 November 2023

42305430R00109